Disability, Inclusion and Teacher Education

Disability, Inclusion and Teacher Education

A Holistic Perspective

Editors
Sailaja Chennat • Alka Behari
Department of Education
University of Delhi, Delhi

SHIPRA

(2022, First Published in 2019)

Rs. 995

ISBN: 978-93-88691-18-5

2026 Imp.

Disability, Inclusion and Teacher Education: A Holistic Perspective

Published by:

SHIPRA PUBLICATIONS
LG 18-19, Pankaj Central Market
I.P. Ext., Patparganj, Delhi 110092, India
+91 11 47322068; 96500 28065, 98105 22367
info@shiprapublication.com
www.shiprapublication.com

Foreword

This is not just one more book on Inclusive Education. Rather, it is a well conceptualised book based on the belief that inclusion is the means to live by the democratic principles of social equity and justice. It also promotes the idea that every individual person in society must be accorded self-worth and dignity and feel valued and safe. This is particularly significant in the context of persons with disability. The editors of the book take us on a virtual tour through the world of disability, locating it in the context of Teacher Education. They have organised the book in six chapters, each dealing with a specific area of disability in a manner which is both informative and engaging. The aim is to help readers to build understanding and perspective on each disability and also an attitude of sensitivity and empathy, alongside. The quest is to prepare professional and humane teachers, in keeping with the goals of teacher education, spelt out in the National Curriculum Framework for Teacher Education (2009).

A very laudable feature of the book is the conscious effort that has been made to locate the discussion in teacher education. Understanding Inclusive education of children with disabilities, and more so, placing them in the realm of teacher education is one of the primary goals of the book which it succeeds in fulfilling, much to the academic joy of the reader. Each of the chapter contributors are persons actively engaged in research and practice with a focus on the distinct disability that they have written about. The conclusive chapter draws implications for teacher education.

As you read through the different chapters of the book, here are some highlights that you would notice – each disability has been discussed as a unit in itself. This is meaningful because very often, the tendency is to club all disabilities together, which, somehow, fails to bring to the forefront the nuances, intricacies and complexities inherent in understanding the uniqueness of each and placing it in the purview of learning and teaching. This, in my view, would also pave the direction towards preparing a set of teachers, who are not only cognitively sound but also equipped with a rich repertoire of skills and attitudes to work towards inclusive education in schools with zest and passion. As a special feature, the book while being descriptive in text, carries visuals of useful assistive devices and case narratives from the Indian context. This greatly enhances the depth of each chapter.

Each time an author attempts to write a book, the language, syntax and the simplicity and transparency with which concepts and ideas are presented make all the difference to its audience appeal. This book fulfils all of these. The audience to whom this book will appeal, to my mind, will consist of teachers, teacher-educators, researchers, students and project and programme staff of non-governmental agencies who work in the field of Education. Each chapter ends with a list of readings which would help the reader to delve deeper into specific areas of interest.

I am pleased to write this foreword not only because the editors, Sailaja Chennat and Alka Behari have been friends and colleagues of mine for many years, but also because I believe that the notion of Inclusive Education of children with disabilities and looking at it from the lens of teacher education has tremendous educative value in the present times. Teachers and students at every level can enrich and strengthen their teaching-learning by understanding the nuances, concepts and dynamics as presented in the different chapters of this book, so thoughtfully developed by the editors. Infact, I am happy to share that the book has, as its antecedent, the contribution of inspirational ideas and perspectives generated during the two-day National Symposium organised jointly by both the editors and myself at the Department of Education, University of Delhi under the aegis of Institute of Advanced Studies in Education (IASE), MHRD, Government of India. The Symposium saw the presence of eminent experts and extensive deliberations among them. The effort was then taken ahead by the Editors who, after the initial completion of preparation of chapters by writers, organised a series of workshops, content and language validation exercises, and then final consolidation of the text.

I would like to thank the joint editors of the book for their invaluable contribution.

Namita Ranganathan,
Head & Dean, Department of Education,
University of Delhi

Preface

This book is an outcome of the culmination of a long and academically rich journey. It began with a two-day National Symposium organised on this area in the Department of Education, University of Delhi in the year 2017 under the aegis of the Institute of Advanced Studies in Education (IASE), a scheme of the Ministry of Human Resource Development (MHRD), Government of India. The Symposium was marked by Lectures and Discussions with renowned experts in the field of Disability as well as Teacher Education. The Symposium was envisioned as a forum to bring together academics, practitioners and researchers to engage in an intensive dialogue and debate aimed at building an informed and nuanced understanding about the field. Dr. Shanti Auluck (Chairperson, Muskaan), Dr. Annie Koshi (Principal, St. Mary's School), Dr. Swati Sanyal (Director, Durgabai Deshmukh College of Special Education), Dr. Varsha Gathoo (Head, Department of Education, Ali Yavar Jung Institute for Hearing Impaired), Dr. Merry Barua (Director and Founder, Action for Autism-National Centre for Autism), and Professor Anupam Ahuja (Head, Department of Education of Groups with Special Needs, NCERT) gave their invaluable contributions that added to the academic rigour and inspiration with which this book was conceptualised, and later written.

The volume comprises six disability areas viz. Autism, Hearing Impairment, Intellectual Impairment, Locomotor Impairment, Specific Learning Disability and Visual Impairment. We appreciate the zeal and expertise of the content writers for taking on the arduous task of amalgamating their ideas to the content related to each disability area.

We would like to thank Dr. Shanti Auluck, (Muskaan), Dr. Swati Sanyal (Durgabai Deshmukh College) and Dr. Bharati (Assistant Professor, Department of Education of Groups with Special Needs, NCERT) for being a part of the content validation process and vetting of the chapters. Their feedback further added quality and essence to the content of each chapter. An in-house workshop was conducted to address this task and bring it to completion. We would like to thank Ms. Shefali Srivastava, research scholar in Language Education from the Department of Education, University of Delhi, for language edition of each chapter. Front cover of this book has been designed by Ms. Chittira S. Panikkar, a graphic designer, working with renowned artist Ms. Bharti Kher. Our sincere thanks are due to her. Our special thanks and gratitude to our friend and colleague of many years, and at present, the Head and Dean, Department of Education (CIE), Prof. Namita Ranganathan for constantly motivating us at every step. She read the draft and gave valuable suggestions.

This book is a result of collaboration as well as dialogue between experts in each area of disability, including teacher educators, teachers, university professors and scholars at the national level; it is expected that it would be of use to practitioners and students across the country. In addition, as per the recent National Council of Teacher Education (NCTE) guidelines, inclusive education has been recognised as a core curricular area of study in all Teacher Education Programmes, hence, this reference book would contribute in building up the discourse on Disability, Inclusion and Teacher Preparation among its readers in a significant way.

Sailaja Chennat • Alka Behari

Contents

1

Understanding Disability and Inclusion

Sailaja Chennat

Inclusion as a Philosophy and Practice

Any society based on democratic principles would have provision of equality of opportunity to its citizens as its primary aim. One of the means of achieving this aim is making the school systems, platforms of equality, equity and justice through inclusive philosophy and practice.

Inclusion is a way of thinking and practising the democratic principles of equality and justice so that every individual of the group feels accepted, valued, and safe. A community that adheres to the philosophy of inclusiveness consciously evolves to meet the changing needs of its members. An inclusive community respects differences among its members and embraces means of enhancing the well-being of every member of the community. In order to ensure well being of each member, societal changes are required at a macro, mezzo and micro levels. At macro level, policy level changes are crucial to make inclusive education a reality. The mezzo level changes to bring about collaborative relationships at the state, district and community level that brings about a culture of inclusiveness is equally important as also the micro level changes at school level, to impact the school ethos, classroom practices and home-school linkages for effective inclusive philosophy and practice.

At the core of most definitions of social inclusion lies the concept of full participation in all aspects of life. Participation creates a sense of responsibility towards others, a community or an institution. Central to the process of inclusion is, efforts to ensure equal opportunities for all, regardless of their background, be it money, class, ethnicity, gender, race, abilities / disabilities or whatever, to enable their full and active participation in all aspects of life, including civic, social, economic, and political. So, logically, social inclusion can be approached as a goal, an objective, and a process.

Diversity as a Premise for Inclusion

If a society is inclusive it means that it understands, accepts and respects diversity, it not only recognises diversity but also embodies it so that each and every member of the diverse society can achieve their full potential in life. Such societal conditions instil in each member a sense of belonging to the community and society at large. Exclusion conversely is a process and a state resulting in lack of access to full participation in mainstream society.

Inclusion as a philosophy and practice cannot be discussed meaningfully unless it is situated in the context of diversity across the members of the group in focus. Diversity in literary terms means differences. But when used in discourse related to people or communities or in social contexts it is more specific; indicates that a group of people comprises individuals who are different from each other in some way or the other or it may also mean collective differences among groups of people which mark off one group from another. Diversity is not simply a descriptive term; it implies an ideological position that values and respects cultural pluralism and supports its preservation within a society; the concept of diversity encompasses acceptance and respect for members of a group; it is loaded with a political perspective positively inclined to equity and justice in society.

It is from the above thread of analysis — diversity loaded with a political analysis—diversity perspective positively inclined to equity and justice in society — that it gets society—that linked to inclusion. Here diversity subsumes the value and respect for pluralism in a social group establishing positive inclination to inclusivity while fostering a feeling of oneness and a sense of belongingness in each of the members of the pluralistic society. It is diversity that brings in the advocacy for equity and justice for each of the persons in a group irrespective of their abilities, disabilities, social status, religion, class, caste and so on and so forth. Another thread of sociological analysis is that it is diversity and exclusion of some who are not like the majority in their group that has given rise to inclusion as a significant discourse in today's academia.

Disability as a Dimension of Diversity

Diversity in a group of people has many dimensions: language, culture, race, ethnicity, skin colour, sex, age, geographic origin, facial features, economic status, educational qualifications and capabilities and disabilities. The important feature of disability is that it is a diversity classification that cuts across all other dimensions like class, caste, race, religion and language. It represents the only minority group that anyone can become a member, anytime in life (Slorach, 2011). This book focuses on disability and the inclusion of children with disability in educational settings.

What is Disability?

Disability is a widely misused and misunderstood concept, as illustrated by the World Health Organization (WHO) definition:

> 'Disability is an umbrella term, covering impairments, activity limitations, and participation restrictions. Impairment is a problem in body function or structure; an activity limitation is a difficulty encountered by an individual in executing a task or action; while a participation restriction is a problem experienced by an individual in involvement in life situations. Thus disability is a complex phenomenon, resulting from the interplay between features of a person's body and features of the society in which he or she lives.'

Disability Groups as Distinct

It is a universal understanding that members of any social group will have varying capabilities and abilities. We also know that all of us who have no disabilities at a particular point in time are temporarily able bodied. Anyone can end up with disability anytime, especially physical disabilities. Many of the persons with disability have been having the disability from birth and others have acquired it through their years owing to various factors. Disability is an inescapable element of human experience.

Furthermore, a group of disabled people is more heterogeneous than those of race, gender, class, and sexual orientation. Disabilities may affect one's senses or one's mobility; they may be static or progressive, congenital or acquired, body form related (affecting the shape of the body) or functional, visible or invisible. These differences converge to the point that any population of disabled people is far from a monolithic; it stands out distinctly with differences that affect the identity of each of its members. For example, people with congenital impairments, say born blind or deaf, are more likely to identify themselves as disabled and reflect pride and self-respect in their social behaviour as compared to those with acquired impairments. Indeed, most people born deaf and well versed with sign language do not consider themselves disabled at all, rather they consider as akin to an ethnic minority, set off the mainstream by their language and culture. Those with acquired impairments are more likely to resist being identified as disabled and spend most part of their life time fighting for an identity of a 'normal person' with medical and rehabilitative support. In any case, the border between the disabled and the abled is less permanent and more permeable than those between races and religions and classes. On the one hand, with the help of bio medicines and rehabilitation, individuals may pass from the status of being disabled to that of non-disabled;

on the other hand, anyone can become disabled at any time and barring sudden or accidental deaths, most people will eventually become disabled to a significant degree as one grows old. In fact we are all temporarily able bodied in a way. So, as a form of social diversity, disability is distinct in its variability, contingency and extent.

Disability and Exclusion

People with disabilities are among the most marginalised groups in the world. They have poorer health outcomes, lower education achievements, less economic participation and higher rates of poverty than people without disabilities (Excerpts from WHO Report, September 2013).

Poverty and social exclusion are inextricably linked, and a major cause of poverty is the lack of employment. For people with disabilities, the situation with regard to employment is far from ideal. Today, the vastness of the free market, the explosion of services like human, welfare, social and educational and professional and the increasing need to be 'intellectually and physically fit' for work, makes people with disabilities economically vulnerable and socially excluded. Therefore, apart from making our educational systems inclusive in philosophy and practice, we need to sensitise employers and employees at all levels to ensure inclusion of people with disabilities.

It is the exclusion of people with disabilities that urges the society to think about and act for their inclusion respecting disability as any other dimension of diversity.

The philosophy and practice of the society with respect to people with disabilities have undergone major changes in the past decades, the capture of which is briefly discussed in the following section.

Societal Responses to People with Disability

History sketches a clear progress of societal response and policy-change from exclusion to inclusion of people with disabilities, through phases of extermination, exclusion, neglect and denial, segregation and integration moving to inclusion. These phases are briefly described below:

Extermination

The intellectually impaired people were referred to by the adjectives, 'feeble-minded', 'invalid', 'imbecile' till as late 18th century. The process of annihilation of the disabled from the mainstream of the general population through killing, mutilating, burning, exiling, abandoning or making them vanish from the scene somehow or the other, were practices in vogue throughout the globe in almost all the ancient civilizations of the world.

Exclusion from a Eugenicist Lens

Eugenics is the study of or belief in the possibility of improving the qualities of the human species or a human population, especially by discouraging reproduction by persons having genetic defects or presumed to have inheritable undesirable traits (negative eugenics) or encouraging reproduction by persons presumed to have inheritable desirable traits (positive eugenics). (Based on Random House Dictionary, 2009).

In the notorious decision of 1927, the US Supreme Court upheld the legality of the forced sterilisation of disabled people. Compulsory sterilisation for people with disabilities became German law in 1933. More than 400,000 people with disabilities were forcibly sterilised (Slorach, 2011).

Institutionalisation

The second phase of Christian era saw the beginning of attempts to stop the abuse of disabled people which was in vogue in the first phase of Cristian era in the medieval period. Disabled children were regarded as those poor souls who are denied opportunities to lead a normal life on account of the annoyance of the Almighty for committing sins; they were thus subjects of sympathy rather than of suspicion or amusement. Influenced by the wave of sympathy and charity, efforts to protect disabled people and establishment of institutions for their welfare and rehabilitation were seen in Europe. Along with these developments, a wide number of institutions, including the mental hospitals called lunatic hospitals, and centres for providing asylums to people with other categories of disabilities were seen mushrooming throughout the globe.

Isolation and Special Schools

The renaissance movement that set off in the 16th century and spread throughout the West in the 17th century was a turning point in the world of disabled people. Contrary to the inhuman approach adopted in the past, there was a faith established in the capacities and capabilities of disabled people. The period of renaissance ignited efforts in the direction of special education for the disabled children. As a major contribution of renaissance and enlightenment movement disabled persons started getting recognised with potential to learn and achieve. Consequently, major efforts were put forth to establish special schools for disabled children segregated from the mainstream settings. It is pertinent to mention here that only deaf, blind and mentally impaired caught the attention of the society till much later after this period.

Segregated Settings — Special Classes in Regular Schools

With the dawn of 20th century, education arena for disabled children witnessed a turning point: moving from the isolated setting of special schools to the segregated settings of special classes within the regular schools. It was the result of a new wave of humanism, coupled with the burning cries for equity of educational opportunities for all children irrespective of their disabilities in the state run schools. By the second half of 20th century the momentum for integration although the philosophy and modalities of which were not clearly spelt out, grew in all strength and vigour in the developed countries, with very little critical analysis of it.

The early phase of this historical milestone saw the establishment of special classes in mainstream schools perceived as 'integration', while recommending that special schools become resource centres for other schools in their neighbourhood areas.

Integration and Inclusion

The era of integration, i.e., educating all students with or without disability in the regular schools represents the modern era and the latest global philosophy in the history of education of children with disabilities. It was after the mid-20th century that this new wave of change that spread across the developed countries, brought in the landmark change in the policy of education of children with disabilities. Upholding the right of each child and providing equity and equality of educational opportunities to all children was the philosophy that led to this new wave of change (Mangal, 2012).

This phase started off with integration, making a limited number of additional arrangements for individual children with disabilities in schools which changed very little overall. It was almost like letting these special children be, rather than being convinced about the philosophy of inclusion and adapting to their needs. This stage slowly evolved into that of inclusion wherein school systems started attempting to bring in radical changes to embrace all children.

In conclusion, it can be stated that from the establishment of first institutions for children who were deaf, blind and intellectually impaired in the early 19th century to the segregated special classrooms in public school systems during the early 20th century (1910s) to the integration or mainstreaming movement of the 1970s to the influential legislative mandates of the last quarter century, many efforts have been put forth to include children with disabilities in regular education settings. The ideal of inclusion has come to symbolise a whole range of efforts to break down distinctions between special and inclusive education in fundamental and dramatic ways.

Perspectives on and Approaches to Disability

Societal perspectives on disability and corresponding approach to disability have changed since the 1970s, prompted largely by the self-organisation of people with disabilities and by the growing tendency to see disability as a human rights issue. Historically, people with disabilities have largely been provided for through solutions that segregate them, such as residential institutions and special schools. Policy has now shifted towards community and educational inclusion, and medically focused solutions have given way to more interactive approaches recognising that people are disabled by environmental factors as well as by their bodies (World Report on Disability, 2011).

Medical Perspective

From a medical perspective, disability is defined scientifically, as a physical, medically diagnosed deficit which handicaps the person concerned. It is impairment-focused, isolating the experience of disability from external influences such as societal attitudes.

In most discourses worldwide the social perspective has overtaken the medical model, whereby cultural environment and attitudes which influence disabled people's societal participation and citizenship status are seen as the hurdle, rather than the physical impairment.

Social Perspective

The social perspective of disability views disability as socially constructed and a consequence of society's lack of awareness and concern about persons who require specific modifications in their environment to live full, productive lives. The perspective, referred to by some as the barriers model, views the medical diagnosis, illness or injury as being no reason for disability. Hence, it has a more human rights as well as contextual dimension. While the social perspective is salient in all contexts, it compromises on the significance of the type and extent of impairment in each individual at the expense of highlighting the socio-political aspects. In the context of a student using wheel chair, unable to access his/her class in a school building with no ramps, the steps in the building and absence of ramp are seen as the barrier disabling the student from the social perspective.

"In the broadest sense, the social model of disability is about nothing more complicated than a clear focus on the economic, environmental and cultural barriers encountered by people who are viewed by others as having some form of impairment—whether physical, sensory or intellectual" (Oliver, 2004).

> Nothing about us without us! By seeing impairment as an ordinary part of life, and disability as the result of discrimination and exclusion, the social model has underpinned efforts to extract disability from the medicalised, 'special needs' ghetto and push for the mainstreaming of disability concerns in all development policies and practices. The social model has also provided a powerful framework for bringing disabled people together in a common struggle for equality and rights. By doing this the social model has promoted the idea that disabled people should be actors in their own lives, rather than passive recipients of care. This equates almost exactly to current thinking on a rights-based approach to development, adopted by government development agencies throughout the world. (Albert, 2004)

Human Rights Perspective

The rights perspective is primarily a fight for access to the privileges people would otherwise have had if they were not disabled. A focus on rights is not a struggle for fundamental social change; rather, it strives to make changes within the existing system. A human rights approach to disability acknowledges the rights of people with disabilities and views social structures and policies restricting or ignoring the rights of people with disabilities as often leading to the discrimination and exclusion of disabled people. A human rights perspective urges society, particularly governments, to actively promote the necessary conditions for all individuals to fully realise their rights.

United Nations Convention on the Rights of Persons with Disabilities (UNCRPD) 2006

The rights based model of disability can be clearly understood from the United Nations Convention on the Rights of Persons with Disabilities (UNCRPD) 2006. The UNCRPD is an international human rights treaty of the United Nations intended to protect the rights and dignity of persons with disabilities. The CRPD sets out to clarify what human rights mean in the context of disability. The first human rights treaty of the twenty-first century, it represents a major step towards realising the right of disabled people to be treated as full and equal citizens. Promoting and protecting the full enjoyment of human rights by disabled people and ensuring they have full equality under the law is what is demanded in this treaty. The convention covers a wide range of areas including health, education, employment, access to justice, personal security, independent living, access to information, etc.

Indian Context—The Rights of Persons with Disabilities (RPwD) Act, 2016

Rights of Persons with Disabilities (RPwD) Act, 2016 was passed in the Parliament replacing the Persons with Disabilities Act (PWD) Act, 1995 in India, in line with the UNCRPD, to which India is not only a signatory but also one of the early countries to ratify. In this Act disability has been defined as an evolving and dynamic concept. The types of disabilities have been increased to 21 and the Central Government has power to add more.

Bio-psychosocial Perspective

The bio-psychosocial perspective of disability is a more contemporary one that situates disability as rooted in an amalgamation of factors at the physical, emotional and environmental levels. This perspective recognises that disabilities are inherited, congenital or due to illness or injury and does take cognizance of the importance of the impact of biological, emotional and environmental issues on health, well-being and function in society.

This approach is consistent with the WHO's revised definitions of disability:

> Disability is an umbrella term, covering impairments, activity limitations, and participation restrictions. Impairment is a problem in body function or structure; an activity limitation is a difficulty encountered by an individual in executing a task or action; while a participation restriction is a problem experienced by an individual in involvement in life situations. Disability is thus not just a health problem. It is a complex phenomenon, reflecting the interaction between features of a person's body and features of the society in which he or she lives. Overcoming the difficulties faced by people with disabilities requires interventions to remove environmental and social barriers.

Inclusive Education

Having discussed the societal responses to people with disabilities and perspectives on disability in the sections above, the following section presents the concept of inclusive education—what is inclusive practice and what is not.

As presented in the opening sentence (page 1), any society based on democratic principles would have provision of equality of opportunity to its citizens as its primary aim. One of the means of achieving this aim is, making the school systems, platforms of equality and justice through inclusive philosophy and practice.

Inclusive education means that all students are welcomed by their neighbourhood schools in age-appropriate, regular classes and are supported to learn, contribute and participate equally in all aspects of the life of the school. All students mean every child irrespective of abilities, disabilities, and socio-economic background, and gender, religious and regional belongingness. Inclusive education is about how we develop and design our schools, classrooms and activities so that all students learn and participate together. The school in the neighbourhood needs to become active sites of inclusive education so that it becomes reality in near future.

Inclusion in education is:

- a process to bring all students together in one classroom and school, regardless of their strengths or weaknesses in any area, and it seeks to maximise the potential of all students;
- a process where diversity in a group with respect to any aspect is appreciated and in which each individual is recognised and respected for what he is worth;
- an effort to make sure that diverse learners—those with disabilities, different languages nd cultures, different homes and family lives, different interests and ways of learning—are taught using teaching learning strategies adapted to individual learning needs;
- is a process that allows every individual to feel accepted, valued, and safe. An inclusive community consciously evolves to meet the changing needs of its members. Through recognition and support, an inclusive community provides meaningful involvement and equal access to the benefits of citizenship
- is a means of enhancing the well-being of every member of the community (Chennat, S., 2017).

What Inclusion means to Students with Disabilities

- Students with disabilities experience school in the same way as their peers without disabilities.
- They experience a school climate wherein they develop a sense of personal belonging and achievement.

- They feel recognised and respected for their abilities
- Students without disabilities learn to be empathetic and sensitive diversity among peers (Chennat, S. 2017).

Following are some of the processes in a classroom and some of the values and beliefs of teachers that lead to classroom ethos being not inclusive:

- Valuing some children more than others in a group.
- Maintaining barriers to some students' participation in the curricula and other activities of school.
- Preserving school policies and practices which are non-responsive to the diversity of learners thus facilitating inequalities.
- Nurturing a mindset that inclusion mostly concerns disabled learners and that school changes made for disabled children will only benefit them.
- Viewing differences between students as problems to be overcome.
- Segregated schooling for disabled learners violates their basic human right to education without discrimination.
- Identifying academic achievement as the main aim of schooling, being prejudiced against the disabled children and being unable to see the abilities and capabilities in them.
- Perceiving inclusion in education as a separate phenomenon not in congruence with inclusion in society. (Chennat, S., 2017)

Perspective of the Book

In order to elucidate the perspective with which this resource book has been developed, it is necessary to delve deeper into disability groups and uncover certain myths about inclusion of children with disabilities which is attempted in the following paragraphs.

Heterogeneity in Disability Groups

Disability is a very general word encompassing extreme heterogeneity of type and severity of impairments like hearing impairments, visual impairments, deaf–blindness, physical disabilities, locomotor and others, intellectual impairments, emotional and behavioural impairments, autism spectrum disorders, speech or language impairments, specific learning disabilities, disability from traumatic brain injury, and so on: From an educational perspective, the type of disability and its degree of severity decide the individualised special education services, including the type of educational settings. The general concept of disability contributes little to the selection of specific treatment approaches or appropriate educational programmes. Moreover, students with exclusively physical disabilities do not usually need special education other than social and architectural accommodations (Hallahan *et al.*, 2009; Kauffman & Hallahan, 2005b).

Multiple Disability and Co-Morbidity

Whenever we refer to a group of children with any one disability, it is generally presumed that all the children in that group would have only the one disability in focus. But, it is possible that there is co-morbidity of that disability with some other less obvious or hidden disability. For example, children with autism might have attention deficit hyperactive disorder (ADHD). There can be also multiple disabilities in a child like deaf-blindness. Such children will have very specific needs that need to be differently addressed, which may be difficult in a regular classroom.

Inclusion for ALL—A Myth

Flowing out from the above points is the clear dictum that children with disability/s form a very diverse group with a spectrum of categories and severity of disability. Those with physical/locomotor disabilities can be placed in regular educational settings with infrastructural adaptations to facilitate their mobility as most of the times these children may not need curricular adaptation. Children with locomotor disabilities may be able to manage their life as efficiently as a nondisabled person at home, school, or community with designed adaptations in buildings, furniture, household appliances and clothing; but their lives are often needlessly complicated because of the environmental barriers. But unfortunately this is not the case for all children with other disabilities. Special, dedicated environments are sometimes necessary for them. The full inclusion of all students, especially, those who are deaf and dependent totally on signing for communication, those with severe Autism Spectrum Disorder and other intellectual disabilities and of those with severe emotional and behaviour disorder is simply not a feasible option.

Significance of Special Schools in the Continuum of Educational Settings

The heterogeneity in groups of children with disability and the wide spectrum of needs of such children have been recognised and accounted for in developed and progressive countries emphasising in principle and practice, the role of special schools in the continuum of educational settings to address the needs of these children. If we really want a politically correct strategy to accomplish inclusion of students with disabilities to the greatest extent feasible, then we cannot run away from confronting difficult educational problems and complex dilemmas, pretending that they do not exist. Differentiated settings imbibing equity and justice to foster the optimal development of children are central to inclusive education as a philosophy and practice. The ideal of an inclusive education does not necessarily correspond to full inclusion of all students in regular schools. Equity in education should not be confused with uniformity.

Visualisation of Inclusive Classrooms

The perspective of this book is a capture of the three threads of analysis presented in the above paragraphs.

It is the bio-psychosocial perspective, of viewing disability as the interplay between the bodily-mental status of the protagonist and the psychosocial environment, from which the editors and the authors of the resource book have presented their understanding and insights. Importantly, the heterogeneity of disability groups with reference to type and degree of disability and the corresponding differentiations required with reference to academic and psychosocial support have been the leading principles for developing the content of this resource book. With the strong conviction that 'inclusion for ALL' is a myth, the inclusive classrooms for which this resource book has been prepared is visualised as having only children with mild to moderate degrees of disability where teachers carry out accommodations and adaptations as required to address the needs of students. In tandem with this conviction is the adherence to the significance of special schools in the continuum of educational settings for children with disabilities, to address the needs of those with severe disabilities.

How the Book is Useful

Regular schools and classroom processes make the context of the book, in which students with and without impairments are taken care of academically and psychosocially. In the groups of students with impairments, only those students with mild to moderate degrees of impairments are expected to be included. The continuum of educational settings from special, to integrated, to inclusive ones is considered pertinent from the perspective with which this book has been developed. This implies the position that special schools are significant in this continuum of educational settings and those students with severe impairment need to be taken care of in special schools by specially trained teachers.

This book attempts to answer the following questions

- What is meant by —? e.g.: dyslexia. Hearing impairment, being deaf, intellectual impairment etc.
- What is the nature of —? e.g.: dyscalculia, autism or how does one identify a child with a specific impairment or, what are the characteristics of a child with a specific impairment?
- What are the needs of a child with a specific impairment that logically flow out from the nature and characteristics of that impairment?
- Given the above needs, what are the academic and psychosocial implications for classroom processes and the school as a whole?
- What are the paedagogic strategies that can help student with a specific impairment in class?
- What is the role of peer group and teachers in the psychosocial well being of child with the disability in focus?
- What is the role of parents of children with impairment in helping their child?
- What is the role of parents of children without impairment in helping child with impairment?
- What are the assistive devices useful for children with a specific impairment and how can they be used for classroom interactions?
- Given the nature and the needs of children with impairments, what are the implications for teacher education programmes?

The perspectives with which the authors have approached the content of each chapter have been explicated to enable easy comprehension by readers. The notion that 'inclusive educational setting is THE option for all children with disabilities of any type and level' has been analysed and the stand of the authors has been clearly explicated in the introduction.

Disabilities covered are:

- Autism
- Hearing Impairment
- Intellectual Impairment
- Locomotor Impairment
- Specific Learning Disability
- Visual Impairment

Each disability has been discussed in depth with a chapter dedicated to each. Reader can get a conceptual understanding about each disability and then go on deeper into the nature and characteristics of students with this disability going on to the paedagogic strategies and the measures for ensuring the psychosocial well being of these students. The role of the others associated with the student with disability, like the parents and the peer group follows sketching the complete picture of the classroom and school ethos surrounding the student with disability. Assistive devices and the ways of their use to help the student with disability are presented at the end of each chapter wherever relevant.

Implications of the nature and characteristics of children with disabilities and the corresponding classroom processes on teacher preparation programmes have been presented in the last chapter on 'Implications for Teacher Preparation'.

It is hoped that this resource book will benefit pupil teachers of B.Ed., B.El.Ed., D.Ed., teacher educators of these programmes, and researchers in the field.

REFERENCES

1. Chennat, S. (2017). *Understanding diversity and inclusion*: Unit 1 Block 1. New Delhi: IGNOU
2. Hans, A. and Patri, A. (Eds.) (2003). *Women, Disability and Identity*, New Delhi: Sage.
3. Hallahan *et al.* (2009). *Exceptional Children: An Introduction to Special Education* (11th Ed.). Boston, MA: Allyn & Bacon.
4. Kauffman, J.M., and Hallahan, D.P. (2005). *Special Education: What It is and Why We Need It.* Upper Saddle River, NJ: Pearson
5. Oliver, M. (2004). *The social model in action: If I had a hammer*, Barnes, C. and Mercer, G. (Eds.). Implementing the social model of disability: Theory and research, Disability Press: Leeds

Web Resources

1. (Ability Junction, 2011). Disability—Human Rights based model versus the Social, Medical and Charity models. Retrieved from http://www.cuts-international.org/cart/pdf/dis-ability_junction_03-2011.pdf)://www.cuts-international.org/cart/pdf/dis-ability_junction_03-2011.pdf
2. Albert, B. (2004). The social model of disability, human rights and development. Retrieved from http://www.enil.eu/wp-content/uploads/2012/07/The-social-model-of-disability-human-rights-development_2004.pdf
3. RPwD 2016. http://pib.nic.in/newsite/PrintRelease.aspx?relid=155592
4. Slorach, R. (2011). Marxism and disability, In International Socialism, 129, 111-136. Retrieved from http://isj.org.uk/marxism-and-disability/
5. UNCRPD (2006). https://www.equalityhumanrights.com/en/our-human-rights-work
6. WHO Report (2013). http://www.who.int/features/factfiles/disability/en/
7. World Report on Disability: http://www.who.int/disabilities/world_report/2011/report.pdf

2

Rethinking Autism

Challenges and Strategies for Inclusion

Supriya Singh

In India, education of children with autism has been a struggle, whether in regular or special school systems. The prominent reasons for this are lacunae existing in various domains such as knowledge about autism, training of teachers, infrastructural modification, conducive environment in schools and the persistence of fallacious myths about autism, among many others. However, it needs to be understood that with an expert teacher, a child with autism could function very well in a regular school, and learn valuable social skills from his/her peers. Currently, schools providing education to children with autism are very few in number.

Introduction

Autism spectrum disorders are lifelong developmental disabilities that can impact how people understand and think what they see, hear and otherwise sense. This can result in difficulties with social relationships, communication and behaviour. Autism is characterised by poor social-communication skills, including poor eye contact, difficulty in maintaining conversations, and lack of developmentally-appropriate peer relationships, as well as the presence of restricted or repetitive patterns of behaviour, such as stereotyped behaviours, hypo- or hypersensitivities, throwing of tantrums and unusual interests. The symptoms of autism typically begin to manifest in early childhood and continue across the lifespan.

Nature of Autism

All children with autism spectrum disorders display difficulties in social interaction and behaviour, but the extent and type of difficulty varies. Some individuals may be withdrawn, or may show hyperactivity and approach people in socially-awkward ways. Others may demonstrate selective attention, resistance to change, limited interests or obsessive behaviours. Majority among them may often respond to sensory stimuli in an atypical manner and may exhibit unusual physical behaviours, such as hand flapping, spinning or rocking. They may also use objects in unconventional ways and demonstrate an unusual attachment toward specific objects.

Types of Autism

Cognitive abilities in people with autism vary between average to above average. Autism may impact each child differently. Each and every learner with autism may have different characteristics of autism. "The term Autism generally refers either to Autistic Disorder or Classical Autism. But it is often used to refer to all Autism Spectrum Disorders. Autism is in fact not 'a disorder'; rather it refers to a spectrum of closely-related disorders, with a shared core of symptoms" (American Psychiatric Association, 2013.) Every individual on the autism spectrum has problems to some degree with social skills, empathy, communication, and flexibility in behaviour. But the level of disability and the combination of symptoms vary tremendously from person to person. In fact, two children with the same diagnosis may differ considerably in their behaviours and abilities. Autism spectrum disorders belong to an umbrella category of five childhood-onset conditions known as Pervasive Developmental Disorders (PDD). Some autism specialists use the terms pervasive developmental disorder and autism spectrum disorder interchangeably.

Case Narration

Read the description about Prankur with autism given below:
Prankur is a five year old boy. Even after reaching the age of three, he had difficulty in expressing his needs; his motor skills did not match those of other children of his age. Development of his communication skills was delayed so much so that even by the age of three he had not spoken any word. Prankur communicated through non-verbal means. He communicated requests primarily by holding the communication partner's hand and placing it on the desired object. When assisted, he used an approximation of the "more" sign when grabbing the hand. He never gave a social smile and did not greet anyone. Prankur did not know how to play with toys and avoided looking at his teacher each time she asked him something. He often appeared to be non-engaged and responded to his name inconsistently.

According to DSM-5 (Diagnostic and Statistical Manual of Mental Disorders, 5th Edition: DSM-5 by American Psychiatric Association), following are the behavioural characteristics of children with autism:

- Do not imitate others
- Treat people like objects
- Lack awareness of the existence or feelings of others
- Do not play with other children
- Get irritated when a guest visits
- Do not feel comfortable with any change in routine, change in room layout or venue of learning/work, change of abode, etc.
- Lack or have unusual emotional responses
- Are socially unresponsive
- Are indifferent or respond negatively to physical affection
- Show no interest in making friends
- Do not understand conventions of social interaction, such as turn-taking
- Do not initiate interactions
- Are socially awkward
- Show little expressive language
- Have delayed language development
- Rarely or never use appropriate gestures
- Show improper use of pronouns, statements and questions
- Say strange things
- Have unusual tone or rhythm of speech
- Are not able to use speech in a meaningful way
- Repeat remarks made by others.

Understanding the Concerns of Children with Autism

Children with autism may experience language and communication related difficulties differently; some are non-verbal while others have extensive language deficits in the social use of language. Children with autism may seem to be living in an imaginary world—a world in which communication is unimportant. This is not an intentional action but rather an inability to communicate and adjust in society. The lack of acceptance in social groups due to limitations in understanding of social norms may exclude them. Some of these limitations are discussed below.

- ***Difficult patterns of Communication:*** Understanding social situations requires processing of language, including both verbal and non-verbal communication, which are often difficult for children with autism. They may not understand important communication gestures, e.g., tone of voice or facial expressions. They tend to face difficulty in using suitable non-verbal behaviours and gestures in social interactions, e.g., making eye contact, using body posture. They may also have difficulty in reading non-verbal behaviours of others. Some autistic children have strong vocabularies and verbal skills, but lack auditory directions or have difficulty in talking about topics other than those of their own specialised interests. When communicating with children with autism, teachers have to use short sentences and say exactly what they mean. For example, the teacher might say, "Sit down and put your hands in your lap," instead of, "Take a seat."

- ***Learning:*** Cognitive features associated with autism also impact each child with autism differently. A child with autism may have problem in paying attention to relevant information and may have limitations in receptive and expressive language, particularly the use of language to express abstract concepts. Another child may have difficulties in concept formation and capacity to share information with others. Children who have autism vary widely in their academic abilities; some children have tremendous difficulty in learning basic skills, including reading, writing and maths. Other children may be gifted in a particular area such as decoding words, but may lack the ability to comprehend meaning while reading. Abstract concepts are also usually difficult. Many children with autism have excellent memories and can quickly learn facts. They have difficulty in transferring newly learned skills from one context to another, which can be improved with appropriate teaching strategies. These strategies must include environmental changes, teaching and prompting strategies, and behavioural contingencies. For example, a teacher might have taught a variety of vocabulary items and children, in general, might have learned more than 50 of these but children with autism would not be able to use any of these words in daily life. Therefore, it is important to provide teaching strategies that connect with their routine as well.
- ***Relationships:*** Positive relationships with people play a significant role in emotional well-being. While children with autism also want friendships and relationships, they may have additional needs regarding initiating them, maintaining them and understanding them. They need people who understand their needs regarding social communication and support them by providing the required encouragement and appreciation. It is a myth that children with autism have no interest in social relationships, as this is not always the case. Many children with autism long for friendships but lack the social skills to initiate and maintain them. Their odd interests and behaviours sometimes alienate them from other children.

Tantrums and behaviour problems may occur when they feel either isolated or bullied.

- ***Sensory problems:*** Children with autism usually differ from others in their sensory experiences. Responses to sensory stimulation may vary from hyposensitivity to hypersensitivity. Environmental stimuli may be disturbing or even painful to children with autism. This may apply to any or all types of sensory inputs. One of the main causes of misbehaviour among children who have autism is that they are over stimulated by their environment. Many children with autism are acutely sensitive to noises, lights, crowds or touch. Classrooms can have soothing neutral colours rather than bright primaries. Natural light and table lamps are preferable to fluorescent tubes. Headphones can be used to block out irritating noises. These are some of the environmental modifications that help these children function to the best of their abilities.

  Self-injurious behaviour: One of the most devastating behaviours seen among people with developmental disabilities such as autism is self-injurious behaviour. The most common forms of these behaviours include: head-banging, hand-biting, excessive self-rubbing and scratching. There are many possible reasons behind a person's self-injurious behaviour, ranging from biochemical to the social environment. Such behaviour reinforces the possibility of their isolation and social exclusion. Self-injurious behaviour sometimes comes from anxiety which may be caused by other factors, such as the inability to express oneself, difficulties with processing sensory information, difficulty in understanding social expectations and fearing situations because they are not understood.
- ***Socio emotional needs:*** The ability to understand and express emotions starts developing from birth. Children with autism often find it difficult to recognise facial expressions and the emotions behind them, copy or use emotional expressions, understand and control their own emotions, understand and interpret emotions. They might lack, or seem to lack empathy with others and find it difficult to describe their feelings. They might say that they do not feel a particular emotion. Children with autism often find it difficult to use emotions to manage social interactions. They might show less concern for others and poor ability to comfort others or share emotions. They need to understand and be aware of self.

Challenges Faced by Children with Autism

Case Narration

Rajan is an 11 year old boy who was diagnosed with autism. He is in IVth standard and has difficulty in maintaining social interactions, and engages in self-talks and pretend plays. He loves to play outdoors with his peers and sibling but faces problems in communicating with other children. He usually becomes frustrated because of his inability to express and communicate his feelings to others which leads to injurious behaviour. He is having difficulty with his morning routine, which further leads to behavioural issues. When Rajan faces these issues, his entire day goes off the track, resulting in trouble concentrating on schoolwork and difficulties in interacting with his peers.

The above narration shows a different pattern of characteristics of child with autism that leads to injurious behaviour. A balance between the needs of the child and modifications in inappropriate behaviour to socially accepted behaviour is required. This can be achieved by adapting educational approaches based on the child's needs by the teachers and the parents. Below are the common academic difficulties in adjustment these children face in daily life.

Acceptance in Social Groups

Acceptance of autism is the first step that teachers and parents can take. Teachers need to understand that the behaviour of a child with autism cannot be changed completely, but can be managed with appropriate teaching strategies. A collaborative student-teacher relationship is based on understanding each other's perspectives and realities. It is important for teachers and school staff to have a clear understanding of the needs and options available for children with autism. It is also important for them to have the required knowledge about the characteristics, strengths and needs that children with autism have. With this understanding and a commitment towards student-teacher collaboration, teachers can create positive and effective educational programmes for students and make them more accepted in classrooms and other social groups.

Sensory Problems in Classroom

Children with autism may feel specific sensory difficulties. For instance, a student who enjoys tactile stimulation may rub saliva on his/her hands to gain desired input. Similarly, a student may engage in aimless running, spinning or crashing. It is also common for children with autism to engage in inappropriate smelling or place inedible objects in their mouths to gain sensory feedback. It may be necessary to create a calm and quiet place in classroom where students can go to relax. Relaxing may mean engaging in repetitive behaviours that have a calming effect on students with autism. In some cases, students who crave certain repetitive movements such as rocking or other self-stimulating behaviours can be provided opportunities where this movement is permitted. These activities should be monitored to ensure safety.

Myths about Autism

Several myths surround the understanding of autism which lead to misconceptions about children with autism in social settings and that in turn lead to inappropriate belief that all individuals with autism avoid eye contact and social contact. The reality is that there is diversity among children with autism, which makes it problematic to use words such as "all" or "every" when describing them. Although social difficulties are common, many individuals with autism display some level of social interest and make some attempt to initiate social interactions. It is also a myth that children with autism have extraordinary skills or talents, e.g., they are able to memorise facts, complete complex mental calculations or compose music. The vast majority of children diagnosed with autism do not possess genius abilities like the characters depicted in the movies. However, most individuals with autism display uneven or scattered skill development. As a result, some skills may stand out in relation to other skills.

Difficulties in Role Playing and Taking Turns in Sports and Cultural Activities

One of the problems faced by teachers is teaching turn taking / following rules of games while playing to children with autism. Being able to play games and take turns is an important social skill and, like most other social skills, it is one that needs to be taught. Turn taking is a difficult skill for children with autism to learn because it relies on one's ability to put oneself in another person's place (empathy), and patience. Neither of these skills is easy for children with autism. Teachers need to help children with autism understand social rules, teach skills several times, and give reminders for the same whenever required.

Difficulties in Communicating

Communicating with others in the classroom and being misunderstood for not being able to explain is another barrier for children with autism. Children with autism may face difficulty in explaining their needs or answering oral questions. In some cases, they may only understand a question if it is posed in a certain way; if the words or the structure of the question are changed, the child with autism might have trouble answering, despite knowing the answer.

Children with autism also find it difficult to re-tell an incident, some being unable to sift relevant from irrelevant information, others may want to narrate stories in detail and some others might not be able to relate to stories or topics that ask them to imagine situations, people or places outside their own realm of experiences.

Challenges faced by Family (Adapted from https://www.sciencedaily.com/releases/2016)

Parents having child with autism experience periods of disbelief and denial, deep sadness and depression after being compelled to accept that their child has autism and self-blame and guilt. Some experience helplessness, feeling of inadequacy, anger, shock and guilt especially in the early periods of realising that their child has autism. Some of the challenges faced by parents of children with autism are: dealing with challenging behaviour of their child with autism; dealing with judgements about their child with autism from others; dealing with advises from others on their role as parents; lack of support from extended family members and community; impact upon the relationship between members of the family. Family members of children with autism are often perceived to experience negative psychological effects which may include higher risk for depression, social isolation and marital discord. The siblings of children with autism have a variety of adjustment and coping difficulties and impaired intimate relationships with their affected sibling.

Fatigue

One of the major issues faced by parents of children with autism is fatigue. It has long been recognised that people with autism produce less melatonin, the hormone responsible for regulating sleep patterns in animals and people. Due to this, the requirement of sleep in these persons is much less compared to others. The result is, while the child may only need to sleep for three or four hours to feel entirely rested, the parents are also compelled to make do with half the recommended amount of sleep on a daily basis—as they have to wake up with their child to ensure that they are safe. This has long-term implications on their overall physical and mental health. The look of exhaustion on their face and eyes is a result of long term sleep deprivation. They are suffering, despite the smile on their face and the spring in their step.

Making Teachers Aware of Child's Behaviour Patterns

The task of ensuring that the teachers are aware of the minute behaviour patterns of their child is a challenge faced by a parent. For example, that Shine taps her foot at 114 beats per minute when she is very upset, or that

John becomes hyperactive and disruptive if he doesn't understand something, has to be clearly made known to the teacher to help the child. To make things worse, by the time that the teacher has got to grips with all of the child's quirks and triggers, as well as those of the rest of their class, the school year is all but over, and the child will be moving into a new class with a new teacher, and the whole cycle starts again.

Dealing with Uncalled—For Advises

Going out with one's child with autism is a terrifying prospect. One of the biggest challenges with that is dealing with meltdown in public wherein the child can be violent, loud and obvious. To the public, however, these behaviours look like a spoilt child's temper tantrums. Comments like, "That child would have got a good spanking from me" and "I would never let my child behave like that in public," do nothing but serve as judgements and belittle the parent. What people do not realise is that the child is entirely unable to regulate themselves during a meltdown, and so it is up to the parent to try to calm them to a point where they can respond and regulate themselves. Going out and managing stress and stimulus levels to a point where meltdowns happen less often in public take time and practice. But the judgemental comments make the parents uncomfortable going out with their child, and the child is then unable to cope with regular activities such as shopping or going on a day trip. This becomes a vicious circle that results in near-complete isolation, which is never a good thing.

Impact of Dealing with Meltdowns

This is one of the most stressful things an autism parent has to contend with. For many parents dealing with their child's meltdown means sustaining cuts and bruises because they keep trying to restrain and calm their child. The emotional impact of such events is enormous; all the same, predicting when a meltdown will occur is impossible.

See these statements from parents which bring out still other challenges that they have to face:

> "My son has had multiple physical problems: chronic constipation, self-harming, food intolerances, epilepsy. Yet it is only the epilepsy which has been taken seriously (although the treatment has been ineffective to date). All his other issues have been dismissed as 'just autism' and there has been a reluctance to offer any kind of investigation or treatment."
>
> "My child with autism refuses to not chew or swallow solid foods at the age of almost five years, insists on liquidising food items, but chews

anything wooden, metal or plastic." Another parent: "Spinning round objects, my child has moved on to smacking one hand on top of the other and biting his hand or fingers to the point where his skin is now leathery as it hasn't had a chance to heal." (https://www.sciencedaily.com/releases/2016)

Case Narration

The following is a narration by a mother having a daughter with autism, working in a Kendriya Vidyalaya School as English PGT. (This article was published in *KVS Newsletter* in 2008).

Autism and the Challenges Ahead
Family Background

My daughter Amritha whom we fondly call Ammu was quite a normal child till she was about three years old. She started all the early childhood milestones at the right age. Of course my husband and I felt that she was a little withdrawn at the age of two and did not speak a lot like the other children of her age. But we consoled ourselves thinking that she was just a quiet, perfect and well-behaved baby. At the age of three when she started her KG, her teachers started noticing that there was something amiss in her behaviour but they could not pinpoint it. By then even I started feeling that something was missing in our relationship—the warmth was not there. But still when I used to cry in front of her she used to get all hot and bothered. Initially she refused to write but after four and a half years she started writing alphabets words and sentences. She picked up arithmetic skills quite fast and people started marveling at her ability in performing addition, subtraction, multiplication and division in no time. All this we achieved in the span of two years i.e. between five and seven years of age. Naturally, people started asking me what the problem was as she was very good at Arithmetic; she never forgot the spellings of new words and could read both Malayalam and English well.

It was during this time that she was diagnosed with Autism, a developmental disorder that affects the brain in the areas of language and social skills, imagination and activity. It is a syndrome known as mind-blindness. Mind reading through gestures, facial expression and tone of voice that comes naturally to an ordinary person totally eludes an autistic person and derails their social development. People with Autism avoid eye contact. They have difficulty in expressing needs, in mastering a language and they tend to repeat an activity many times over. Typically Autism appears in the first three years of birth and is difficult to identify. Even a CT scan will not reveal much. From one in 10,000 children 10 years ago, the prevalence now is three to four per 1000 live births.

Till Class IV my daughter went to a normal school but after that the real problems started. The tantrums, which were not so frequent before now became a common occurrence and the teachers found difficulty in managing her. We could not understand the reason for this sudden change. Maybe a lot of factors were responsible. She was growing older and the pressure of a normal school was too much for her. I too could not devote so much of my time as of old because I became a mother again. My son is now 10 years old. Even though both of them have petty fights like any other normal siblings they share a good relationship. Somehow, I feel she is more tolerant towards her brother than towards anyone else. We took her away from a normal school as she could not cope up and now she is in a resource room at a special school where they engage her with games like jigsaw puzzles and training in social skills. She loves music especially melodies and so she is trained at home by a music teacher. She looks forward to these sessions and keeps on asking us when the next class is.

Even after prolonged years of study, causes for Autism are still being debated and remain a profound mystery. Eighty per cent of autistic people are male, meaning the risk is five times greater for boys. Scientists are yet to explain this disparity. Many experiments have pointed to the genetic link; environmental factors such as toxin levels in the blood, mercury due to vaccines and pesticides and also due to exposure to pitocin, the synthetic version of the brain chemical (oxytocin) that helps induce labour. But no conclusion has been reached upon. Whatever the cause, Autism, the third most common developmental disorder, is also one of the most misunderstood medical illnesses. It was only in the 1960's that the world began to identify symptoms specific to this disability.

Autistic Savants

Autism has more than one face. Some are mentally retarded, some suffer from epilepsy but there are others who are capable of functioning at a higher level. These 'Autistic Savants' can memorise a list of dates and numbers or measure the exact height of a building by glancing at it. Some show exceptional skill in areas such as art, music and excel in certain mental tasks. The movie 'Rain man' is centred on such an 'Autistic Savant'. Some of the exceptionally lucky ones are able to live independently with a small job, thus carving a niche for them, physically and mentally.

My family has gone through several stages of depression, despair and hope, anger, denial and guilt. There was the usual rigmarole of hospitals, therapists, psychologists and training methods thinking that my daughter was going to get better and become a normal child. But once we abandoned that idea and started accepting her as she was, being able to laugh over her little pranks without despairing, things became a lot easier. Now we have accepted and resigned ourselves to our fate. God has given us the courage to face as well as take up the challenges offered by Autism in a positive way. In spite of the dark clouds hovering above, I feel that we have now become the happy family we set out to be right from the beginning.

Finally, I would like to quote a few lines from a poem by Edna Massionilla, which has inspired me a lot and has given me the courage to live on.

Heaven's Very Special Child

A meeting was held, quite far from earth!
It's time again, for another birth
Said the angels, to the lord above
This special child will need much love.
His progress may be very slow,
Accomplishments he may not show.
And he'll require extra care
From the folks he meets down there.
He may not run or laugh or play,
His thoughts may seem, quite far away
In many ways he won't adapt,
And he'll be known as handicapped.
So let's be careful where he's sent,
We want his life to be content.
Please, Lord, find the parents who
Will do a special job for you.
They will not realize right away
The leading role they are asked to play,
But with this child sent from above
Comes stronger faith and richer love,
And soon they will know the privilege given
In caring for their gift from heaven.

Challenges faced by Siblings of Autistic Children

The siblings of individuals with autism have a variety of adjustment, coping difficulties and impaired intimate relationships with their sibling having autism. Different studies pertaining to parental characteristics relay a concern for the perceived stress in the health of family environment. The studies on sibling characteristics reveal a variety of influences on personality traits and they accentuate that an interaction of variables comprise the environment of families with persons of autism (Smith *et al.*, 2010). Research also indicates that siblings of children with autism are at risk of bearing the psychological and emotional brunt of growing up alongside a child with behavioural difficulties. Many siblings have felt that their parents perceived their needs as being secondary, with more time and attention given to the child with autism. Whilst they may have a deep love for their sibling, they may also harbour feelings of resentment at the amount of time their parents are spending with the child with autism, and feel that they are being treated unfairly. Thus, feelings of anger, embarrassment and guilt are as normal as is feeling very protective of their sibling. Siblings of children with autism are significantly more likely to experience depression than the general population. Apart from psychological problems, exhaustion may affect siblings who may be responsible for domestic tasks and physical care. Problems may also arise when the increased parental expectations are not accompanied by increased parental time or attention (Gupta and Singhal, 2005).

Addressing the Challenges

There is a dire need to address the challenges of children with autism. Teachers and school staff can make conscious efforts by modifying lessons and classrooms to address the needs of these children. Often, very simple adjustments are required. This section presents ways in which the challenges mentioned above can be addressed.

Teacher Preparation

A teacher may facilitate improvement in the behaviour of a child with autism by formally and systematically assessing conditions that bring about inappropriate behaviours. Understanding the origin of problematic behaviours enables a teacher to help the child learn new skills that will help him/her to achieve the desired result. The teacher should have a holistic understanding of children with autism, and be equipped with strategies to assist in their successful inclusion. Teachers should recognise that a child with autism may want to interact, but may not know how to initiate the communication. Teachers can help the student learn skills for initiating conversation, changing the topics of the conversation when necessary, rehearsing strategies for social interactions. People still believe that children with autism behave in peculiar and disruptive ways and are dependent on others. Teachers' perceptions about autism as a disability and about children with autism in the classroom play a critical role in their successful inclusion. Teachers with positive perceptions tend to put forth more effort and time to help children become successful (Chakrabarti, S., & Fombonne, E., 2005). If teachers have exposure to different disabilities, they become more comfortable and positive about inclusion of students with disabilities in class. Teachers need basic knowledge and skills required to facilitate inclusion of children with autism in class. More information regarding autism, transactional strategies and processes to be followed for family collaboration; more case and field-based experiences for pre-service teachers; and increased access to current research on best practices and teaching strategies for supporting students with autism in the classroom are all significant to enrich the knowledge of teachers. Sensitisation programmes about autism and other disabilities can be organised in schools for teachers, other staff members and children in different forms of activities, excursions, helping meetings and through sports and cultural activities. One of the most effective ways through which teachers can prepare for the inclusion of children with autism is to develop an understanding about the disorder by obtaining information from reliable sources. It is also important to gain knowledge about strategies for inclusion of children with autism. This can be achieved through updating their knowledge by reading, seeking out professional development experiences, talking to or observing teachers with experience and teaching students with autism.

a. Classroom Modifications

Children with autism may require extra help because of sensory difficulties. Children with autism who experience great difficulty with fine motor tasks may be more successful in using computers to complete written assignments. Some students become distracted by irrelevant information, e.g., page numbers, lines, pictures. It may be necessary to eliminate extraneous details from books and worksheets. Some students find glossy surfaces distracting. It may be necessary to adapt books and desktops to give surfaces a matte finish. In some situations, it can be helpful to define the physical space associated with a particular activity in a concrete manner. Children with autism will benefit from a quiet, distraction-free learning area. Because of their sensory issues, too much noise, movement, bright colours and pictures may cause difficulty for some children. Similarly, if using pictures to teach, teachers should avoid complicated pictures or pictures with too much information. These could be difficult for a child with autism to understand. For example, children with autism may be more successful during group activities that are completed on the floor if a specific area is defined for them. Mats or squares can be provided during activities.

b. Learning Accommodations

One of the most effective approaches to teaching children with autism involves the use of visual aids. Students often demonstrate relative strengths in concrete thinking, rote memory and understanding visual-spatial relationships, and difficulties in abstract thinking, social cognition, communication and attention. Pictographic and written cues often help children with autism to learn and communicate. One advantage of using visual aids is that children can use them for as long as they need to process information. Teachers often need to break complex tasks down into sub-skills to ensure successful learning for children with autism. Teachers need to understand the thinking process and behaviour of children with autism if they realise that they think differently and may miss significant details. For example, while learning about Newton's laws of motion, the child with autism may appear more interested in the example of train or any other vehicle rather than on the statement of the laws. Children with autism demonstrate these difficulties in a variety of observable ways. They may engage in excessive or inappropriate laughing or giggling. Some children with autism may play near others, but might not share and take turns, while others may withdraw entirely from social situations.

Psychosocial Accommodations

Children with autism have significant challenges in three broad areas: interacting with other people, verbal and non-verbal communication, and flexibility in thought and action. Teachers at school can play an important role in helping children with autism move towards actualising their abilities. They should thus be aware of the children's abilities and nurture them, while not insisting on goals for which the children are not ready. Children with autism also need to feel safe in their learning environment (safety needs). If they feel vulnerable, if they are afraid of making mistakes or of not fitting in with the peer group, they will be less able to learn. Communication is needed for developing understanding and acceptance at a time when the child is filled with emotions. Teachers can encourage independence by encouraging the child consistently to be independent. This will prepare her/him better to participate in a wide range of activities, events, and relationships in life with less need for additional support. Teachers can empower children with autism by encouraging them to become responsible towards their own learning and for establishing social relations with peers. Skills such as saying 'hello' first or consulting visual reminders/schedules when in doubt, regarding what should be done next, have long lasting benefits.

Peer Counseling

Peer counseling is essential for children with and without autism. It includes teaching them the necessary skills of striking and developing friendships, and respecting each of their friends with their differences. It is important to make them aware of the characteristics of autism to enable them to accept their peers with autism. Engaging in social interactions with peers is essential for their effective learning. For this, counseling of peers is vital. Classmates frequently misinterpret the behaviour or mannerisms of children with autism due to lack of awareness. For example, it is common for peers to assume that children with autism are unfriendly when they do not respond to questions or greetings. Some students assume that echolalia is intended to mock others or that it is a result of "being allowed to do whatever they want to". Peer counseling includes making them aware about the difficulties and challenges faced by children with autism, and the ways in which they can communicate with and play with these children. It is important to help peers develop insights into the possible causes of behaviours of students with autism often display. Dispelling myths about autism can help peers become more accepting. Making peers aware of the ways of involving and interacting with children with autism will have implications for healthy social relationships between them.

Peers in inclusive classrooms can help by teaching concepts to other children who may require additional learning support. Peers can work better in pairs or groups which can help them understand more quickly.

Teaching another student motivates students to first understand the concepts themselves and while teaching, their knowledge of those concepts strengthens which benefits them even more. This can be done in the house activities during cultural sessions. It will eventually decrease the instances of bullying of the child with autism by other children. Teachers can provide opportunities for more communication with other peers in the class. For example, involving students with autism in shared learning arrangements, pairing them up with other peers for outdoor playing or helping other learners with disabilities in the playground and during other unstructured times, and facilitating involvement in extracurricular activities can go a long way in helping children with autism. Pairing with older learners during house activities makes them more aware and helps in their adjustment to various social situations, provided that the older learners extend the necessary support for success.

Peers often feel hesitant to interact with children with autism for the fear of saying or doing something wrong. The best way to help them overcome this fear is to provide them with relevant information and practical suggestions (action points) to deal with children with autism, such as to be gently persistent during interactions, to repeat questions and comments, to offer cues and assistance rather than giving answers. Let us read the narration given below in the context of this discussion.

Case Narration

Saransh is studying in VIth class in a regular school. He had delays in reaching developmental milestones of early childhood; he had delayed speech, with difficulties in social interactions. As a young child, Saransh's play was repetitive with seeming unawareness of others. He did not like to be touched or to be close to others. He often used his sense of smell to investigate objects and had an unusual interest in small objects, such as keys or switches. When Saransh was six years old, his mother consulted a clinical psychologist who diagnosed him as autistic with mild characteristics. At the age of 11, Saransh still has behaviours that require significant support. His teachers provide support in the classroom with modified assignments and an individualised visual schedule. The classroom routines include reinforcers and rewards to maintain appropriate behaviour. Saransh is highly sensitive to changes in the given schedule and becomes aggressive during any unexpected last moment changes. The behaviours of concern to the teachers are banging on the desk or table, head-banging, agitated response if others fail to use specific cues, ignoring adult direction, yelling and throwing objects. These behaviours pose a threat of physical harm to him and disrupt the orderly functioning of the classroom.

Saransh's academic skills are improving with the use of modified worksheets and ICT in learning: for example, use of spelling correction software. Most academic tasks can be modified for Saransh. Saransh likes to make detailed drawings, but tends to focus on the same subjects, usually cars and trucks. He enjoys listening to music, but does not participate in music activities that require interacting with other students. The teacher pairs Saransh in all group activities with another boy. They share their work and they play together. They play vocabulary games, puzzle games during breaks. Saransh's friend became both a play partner and a mentor for him. Saransh has been showing gradual improvement in communication skills and academic work.

The above narration presents the impact of peer help and the importance of early identification. Saransh's early identification helped in his early specialised therapies and interventions which helped him to adjust in an inclusive classroom.

Attitude of Parents and Society

Parental and societal awareness and understanding about autism needs to be enhanced tremendously. Individuals and families living with children with autism, often have poor understanding and resultant unsympathetic attitudes towards them based on stereotypical beliefs such as 'autism only affects children', 'all people with autism are geniuses' or that 'they lack empathy'. Autism can have a profound effect on individuals and families, but understanding and support can make enormous differences. Parents need to accept the disability first in order to provide early intervention for successful inclusion.

Case Narration

Keshav was diagnosed with autism when he was four years old. Before that, his parents experienced some odd behaviour, such as staring at the television, repeating dialogues from television shows over and over. From the time he was nine or ten years old, he expressed obsession with different cars, and he collected a lot of information regarding model, make, year, special features, etc. about cars. During his early childhood, he had delay in speech development and exhibited an obsession with telephones. Each time he saw a phone, he would pick it up as if he was answering, and say to no one, "Hello! H...bye-bye!" and hang up. His parents were told by professionals that he would have difficulties in learning to read and write, going to school without assistance, or even talking. But they started special education for him in his early years. He was provided speech therapy and occupational therapy sessions which seemed to help him fairly well with academics. Now he is a successful graduate and an automobile engineer. Though knew things were not going to be easy, his confidence made this happen positively. Moreover, parental acceptance of autism helped them manage autism efficiently.

Parents of children with autism need to understand that finding suitable strategies to manage autism is far more important that finding its root cause. One has to accept that autism cannot be cured but can be managed with proper educational strategies, counseling and most importantly, with the cooperation of care givers.

Use of Technology

Technology has been used as tool for learning by children with and without disabilities, but it is especially beneficial for children with autism. "The rise of ICT and Internet pushed and extended the development of the use of technologies in education, too". (www.autisminternetmodules.org). New applications such as Android devices, 3D Google, projectors, motion sensing devices and the like, provide the potential for using computers in education.

Learning Process for Children with Autism

Children with autism now share their thoughts and feelings with the help of social networking sites. Teachers can promote the use of technology in classrooms. They can pair up children with or without autism during computer sessions for better peer support and learning. Use of software especially created for teaching-learning processes can be highly beneficial. For instance, word processing as a cognitive tool includes the ability to revise a text, produce clear and readable content as well as to edit and correct a text, which is important for both writing and speaking. Word processing is also helpful for children with autism to type correctly. Word prediction software is another example of computer-based application that can be very helpful for children with communication difficulties. Word prediction function suggests a list of words starting from one or several letters when a student presses on the keyboard. When the expected word appears, the student can easily select it thereby avoiding the uncertainty and frustration related to language-based difficulties.

There are many other useful applications launched especially for children with autism. One of the apps, "Avaz", which can be installed on iPads, is helping children communicate with ease. It helps children who have a problem with speech. Avaz uses picture symbols and high-quality voice synthesis to help users create messages and develop language skills.

Children with autism can follow online discussions initiated by the teacher. They can share and exchange ideas using keyboard. They can type the discussions and their queries using keyboard and feel more independent in expressing themselves. Online engagement further improves social interaction. Skills learnt in a classroom can be practised in an online setting such as blog. This might demonstrate unexpected social skills, which are not practised in face-to-face meetings.

Conclusion

Although raising a CwA can be extremely stressful and life changing, parents are able to find resilience in their child and are able to recognise positive ways in which autism has impacted their lives. An inclusive school when accommodating a CwA should work on many aspects like education and socio-emotional well-being and their safety; policy implementation and practices; setting up of teaching teams and using collaboration as a strategy; soliciting parents', teachers' and students' views and voices as sources of insight; making academic access possible through adaptations and accommodations; mediating participation of all stakeholders; familial and peer support. The therapies and interventions of CwA vary as a function of age and the nature of challenges in communication, social skills, empathy and sensory vulnerability that they face. Autism cannot be cured, but teachers, peers, parents and family members can together help these children to cope with the challenges and live their life with dignity and a smile.

REFERENCES

American Psychiatric Association. (2013). Diagnostic and Statistical Manual of Mental Disorders, DSM 5. Washington, DC: American Psychiatric Association

Barua, M. (Ed.) (2006). *Curriculum and Teaching DSE ASD Manual*. New Delhi: Kanishka Publishers.

Chakrabarti, S. and Fombonne, E. (2005). "Pervasive developmental disorders in preschool children: Confirmation of high prevalence". *American Journal of Psychiatry*, 162(6): 1133-1141.

Daley, T.C. (2004). "From symptom recognition to diagnosis: Children with Autism", *India Journal of Social Science and Medicine*, 58(7): 1323-1335.

Gupta, A. and Singhal, N. (2005). "Psychosocial support for families of Children with Autism", *Asia Pacific Disability Rehabilitation Journal*, 16(2).

Smith, L.O. and Elder, J.H. (2010). "Siblings and family environments of persons with Autism Spectrum Disorder: A review of the literature", *Journal of Child and Adolescent Psychiatric Nursing*, 23(3): 189-195.

Web Resources

https://www.sciencedaily.com/releases/2016 (Challenges faced by Family)

www.autisminternetmodules.org (AIM) Free interactive empirically-based training modules on autism topics. Presented in small increments with pre/post testing

3

Rethinking Hearing Impairment

Issues, Concerns and Inclusive Practice

Sangeeta Singh

Understanding Hearing Impairment

Hearing is one of the five senses that allows us to perceive sound. Hearing impairment, or hearing loss, occurs when one loses part or all of one's ability to hear. Other terms that are used to refer to hearing impairment are deaf and hard of hearing. Hearing impairment is classified in terms of severity and type of hearing impairment. The severity of the hearing impairment is categorised based on the minimum sound that can be heard with the better ear. The higher the decibel (dB), the louder is the sound. With mild hearing impairment, the minimum sound that can be heard is between 25 to 40 dB. People at this level cannot hear soft noises and may have trouble following conversations in noisy settings. Intensity of sound is expressed in decibels. A decibel (dB) is one tenth of bel (A bel is a unit of measurement named in the honour of Alexander Graham Bell).

Intensity Level of Common Sounds

0-1 dB	equivalent to the faintest sounds that can be heard
10 dB	Rustling of leaves
20 dB	whispering, ticking of a watch
30 dB	quiet conversation, soft whisper
40 dB	quiet office, living room, bedroom away from traffic
60 dB	air conditioner at twenty feet, conversation [at one metre], sewing machine,
80 dB	heavy city traffic [25-50 feet], alarm clock at two feet, factory noise, vacuum cleaner, heavy truck
100 dB	speeding express train, some car horns at five metres, farm tractor
120 dB	amplified rock concert in front of speakers
140 dB	a gunshot blast, jet plane take-off at close range [approximately 200 feet]

Source: http://wordinfo.info/unit/620/ip:1/il:D

Hearing impairment affects children of different age groups. Malfunctioning of the hearing mechanism and damage to any part of hearing apparatus can lead to hearing loss in children. As a consequence of hearing loss, children experience delay in speech development, problems in social interaction and face educational challenges. Hearing loss results in delayed speech and language development which further affects communication skills and academic achievement of children with hearing impairment (CwHI). The earlier the hearing loss occurs in a child's life, the more serious will be the effects on the child's development. There is no single intervention service and educational programme that can cater to the needs of every child with hearing impairment because of the diversity among them in terms of degree of hearing loss, age of onset, type of hearing loss and cause of hearing loss. Therefore, CwHI have different educational and social needs depending on the nature of hearing impairment.

CwHI can be classified into several categories based on various criteria mentioned below:

Degree of Hearing Loss: Degree of hearing loss refers to severity of hearing loss. These losses may be ranged in a continuum from mild to profound. The description of hearing loss is typically given in terms of decibel (dB) loss in the better ear. The higher the decibel level, the louder the noise. An individual's hearing loss is tested across several frequencies. Children with hearing impairment can be classified into seven categories on the basis of their hearing loss as per Goodman's (1965) classification.

Classification	*Hearing loss range (in dB)*
Normal Hearing	10 to 15
Slight Hearing Loss	16 to 25
Mild Hearing Loss	26 to 45
Moderate Hearing Loss	46 to 55
Moderately-severe Hearing Loss	56 to 70
Severe Hearing Loss	71 to 90
Profound Hearing Loss	and more

Intensity of sound is expressed in decibels. A decibel (dB) is one tenth of a bel. A bel is a unit of measurement named in the honour of Alexander Graham Bell.

Hearing loss affects people of all ages. There are many factors that are responsible for causing hearing loss. Whether the hearing loss is permanent or temporary also depends on the part of the ear affected. The three basic categories of hearing loss are: conductive hearing loss, sensorineural hearing loss and mixed hearing loss.

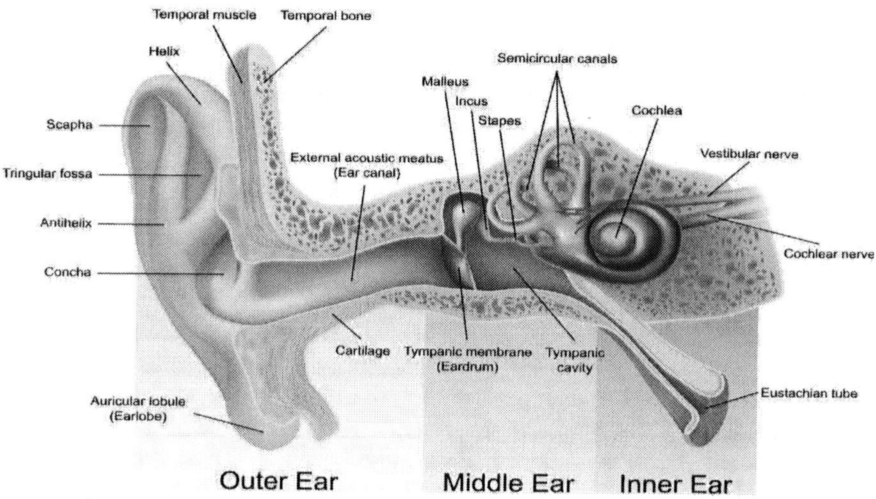

Fig. 3.1: Structure of Human ear

Source: http://simplebiologyy.blogspot.in/2014/11/human-ear-outer-ear-middle-ear-inner-ear-hearing.html

Conductive Hearing Loss: Conductive hearing loss is caused by obstructions in the outer or middle ear which is the conduction pathway for sound to reach the inner ear. It prevents the sound vibrations to reach the auditory nerve causing a loss in conduction. The obstructions can be caused by fluid in the middle ear from cold or allergies, ear infection, excessive amount of ear wax, hole in the ear drum and foreign body in the ear canal. Conductive hearing loss can often be corrected medically or surgically.

Sensorineural Hearing Loss: It results from damage to the inner ear (cochlea) or the nerves which are pathways for sound vibrations from the inner ear to the brain. Mostly, it cannot be corrected medically or surgically. It may lead to permanent hearing loss. Children with sensorineural hearing loss find difficulty even in hearing very loud noise.

Mixed Hearing Loss: It occurs when a conductive hearing loss happens in combination with sensorineural hearing loss. There is impairment in outer, middle and inner ear.

Prelingual and Postlingual Hearing Loss: CwHI can have prelingual hearing loss or postlingual hearing loss depending on the age at which they lost their hearing power. Prelingual deaf are those children who lost their hearing before acquiring speech while postlingual deaf children become deaf after developing speech.

Congenital and Adventitious Hearing Loss: Hearing loss which occurs before or at birth is called congenital hearing loss and hearing loss that occurs after birth is known as adventitious hearing loss.

> Note: All congenital hearing loss is pre-lingual but not all pre-lingual loss is congenital.

Bilateral and Unilateral Hearing Loss: Bilateral hearing loss refers to hearing loss in both ears. Unilateral hearing loss means hearing loss in one ear while other ear is normal.

According to World Health Organization (WHO), a person who is not able to hear as well as someone with normal hearing—hearing threshold of 25 dB or better in both ears—is said to have hearing loss. It classifies people with hearing loss into two broad categories. 'Hard of Hearing' refers to people with hearing loss ranging from mild to severe and 'Deaf' to those who have profound hearing loss, which implies very little or no hearing.

According to the RPWD Act 2016, the term "Hearing impairment" can be understood as follows:

- "Deaf" refers to a person having 70 dB hearing loss in speech frequencies in both ears.
- "Hard of hearing" refers to a person having 60 dB to 70 dB hearing loss in speech frequencies in both ears.

> **Facts about Sign Language**
>
> Sign Language is a visual-spatial language.
> It has its own grammatical and linguistic structure comparable to those of spoken languages.
> The grammar of sign language relies on space, hand shape and movements.
> It is used by the people of Deaf community for communication.
> The language also has non manual component — facial expressions, body movements — that play an important linguistic role in constructing visual-spatial utterances.
>
> *Source: Tomaszewski*, P. (2001). Psychology of Language and Communication, 5 (1), 67-80

Though persons with hearing threshold of below 60 dB are not considered hearing impaired as per the Indian RPWD Act 2016, it has severe impact in their educational and social development. The chapter will discuss the issues and concerns of CwHI who have hearing loss below 60 dB in addition to those of "deaf" and "hard of hearing". Generally, hard of hearing people, which include individuals with mild to moderate hearing loss, can understand speech using assistive devices such as hearing aids. Deaf children need more extensive support, such as sign language interpreters, teachers who know sign language and extensive technology. This chapter will focus on CwHI who can benefit by the use of assistive devices and use their residual hearing to understand oral classroom transactions. This is not to say that deaf children cannot be included in regular schools. Inclusion of deaf children would need intensive efforts, including provision of sign language interpreters, teachers knowing sign language, educational resources as per the specific needs of CwHI and knowledge of sign language among hearing peers. In India, we still have a long way to go to fulfill the needs of deaf children for their proper inclusion in regular schools.

Communication Needs of Children with Hearing Impairment (CwHI)

Communication is a big challenge for CwHI. Depending on the nature of deafness, different approaches to communication can be used for the development of desired communication skills. Children with pre-lingual hearing loss suffer greater disadvantage in language acquisition and development of speech as compared to those who suffer hearing loss after language and speech development. Majority of CwHI are born to hearing parents who have to face hard times while making decisions on communication choices for their CwHI. There are various factors that impact the language acquisition of CwHI. These include degree of hearing loss, age of onset, hearing status of parents and home environment. A child will learn language only if language input is present in the environment. Therefore, one must communicate with CwHI whenever they are around. If CwHI are in an environment of limited language exposure and opportunities for communication, they will learn words more slowly. This will cause a delay in language development. Thus, CwHI have difficulties in language acquisition and incidental learning.

CwHI use a variety of methods to communicate, such as speech, speech/lip-reading, gestures, sign language and combination of speech and sign language. Every child with hearing impairment has different needs for communication. Therefore, it is necessary for teachers and parents to recognise their communication needs for optimum language development.

What is total communication?

Total Communication (TC) is the philosophy of educating children with hearing loss that incorporates all means of communication: formal signs, natural gestures, finger spelling, body language, listening, lip-reading and speech. The goal is to optimize language development in whatever way is most effective for the individual child. Total Communication is truly a philosophy rather than a methodology.

Source: Communication considerations A-Z http://www.handsandvoices.org

Approaches to Communicate with CwHI

- *Oral/Aural communication approach:* It discourages the use of sign language and other manual methods of communication. CwHI are expected to use their residual hearing in order to have access to spoken language. Attempts need to be made to create suitable environment to develop residual hearing and speaking abilities. This includes amplification of sound, auditory training, lip reading and use of technological aids.
- *Manual communication approach:* It encourages the use of sign language, gestures, finger spelling and cued speech for developing the desired communication skills among CwHI.

Myths and Misconceptions about CwHI

There are several myths that are associated with CwHI. These myths increase the barriers in the path of development of children with hearing impairment. Directly or indirectly, these barriers affect the pedagogy of teaching CwHI. Therefore, teachers, parents and professionals associated with CwHI must have knowledge of facts related to hearing loss, characteristics of CwHI and the latest technology that can help them to function optimally. In the following table let us look at the existing myths and facts about CwHI:

Myths	*Facts*
A child's hearing loss cannot be identified unless s/he is three years old	Hearing loss can be identified even in newborns
Children outgrow hearing loss as they grow up	Most children who have damage in the inner ear have a permanent hearing loss which cannot be outgrown
Hearing aids/ cochlear implant should be fitted when the child grows old enough to handle it	There should be no gap between the identification of hearing loss, fitment of hearing aids and language intervention
Children with hearing loss should attend special school	Special school placement is an intervention strategy and not mandatory
Children with hearing loss are a homogenous group i.e. all of them exhibit similarities in terms of educational challenges	No two children are alike and hence no two children with hearing loss can be alike
Hearing impairment can be 'cured' by using a hearing aid	Hearing impairment is not a 'disease' to be cured

(*Contd.*)

Myths	*Facts*
Teachers should speak loudly while talking to a child with hearing impairment	Speaking loudly to a child using an amplification device such as a hearing aid or a cochlear implant can cause pain in the child's ears, distort the sounds and also damage the speaker's voice
All children with hearing impairment need curricular adaptations	There is a growing trend amongst children with hearing impairment to appear for all scholastic subjects without opting for educational concessions
Children with hearing impairment have lesser cognitive abilities	Children with hearing impairment have been found to be at par in many cognitive domains, such as visual spatial relations, bodily kinaesthetic intelligences, etc.
Children with hearing impairment cannot attend college	Many children with hearing impairment have been academically successful in higher education

Source: Gathoo, V. (2016, March). I have a deaf child in my class, what do I need to know? Symposium on Disability, Mental Health, and Teacher Preparation conducted at University of Delhi, Delhi.

Behavioural Manifestations of CwHI

Since a major part of learning takes place in classrooms, it is necessary for teachers to understand the needs of children with special needs. Children with hearing impairment manifest particular kind of behaviours which a teacher must observe, understand and keep in mind while teaching in the classroom. Some of the behaviours exhibited by CwHI in the classroom which can help teachers to identify them are as follows:

- They often make mistakes while speaking. They either leave certain sounds or substitute one sound with another.
- They try to listen while looking at the speaker.
- They may act dramatically to express themselves when they are happy, sad, excited etc.
- They throw tantrums to gain attention.
- They may not respond when their name is called out from behind, other rooms and distant places.
- They complain of earaches and discomfort in the ear.
- They may have frequent ear discharges and ear infections.
- They use limited vocabulary to express their views.
- They may not answer questions and sometimes answer incorrectly.

- They are often not able to follow oral instructions during group activities in physical education classes and imitate their hearing peers.
- They ask for the instructions repeatedly.
- They watch the lips of the speaker closely.
- They speak either too softly or too loudly.
- They feel reluctant to participate in oral activities.

Screening and Assessment

School age screening is an essential tool for early identification of hearing impairments. It allows the referral to specialists who provide interventions for the cognitive, social, emotional and language development of CwHI. Students with unilateral and less severe hearing impairment or those who suffer hearing loss later in life are often not identified or sometimes misdiagnosed because of their behaviour in the classroom. For example, a child may ask the teacher to repeat things frequently. The teacher might feel that the child is doing so to seek attention or to distract other students in the class. Therefore, it is crucial to ensure that CwHI are identified and diagnosed properly. It will help teachers to take proper initiatives for planning teaching strategies and classroom adaptations based on their needs.

A study was conducted in Tamil Nadu to estimate the prevalence of hearing impairment in school children aged 8 to 14 years in schools. It was found that among 700 school children of age 8 to 14 years, 216 (30.9%) have hearing impairment. The study urged to carry out regular check-ups for ear diseases and hearing assessment at school level to prevent hearing loss (Norman, Chandran and Dhandapani, 2016). Hearing loss has drastic impact on language and educational outcomes of CwHI. Therefore, early identification and management through hearing screening programmes is essential. Teachers should be given proper education on how to identify ear diseases and to refer students to suitable health facilities if need arises.

Inclusion of CwHI in Regular Classrooms

Inclusion of CwHI necessitates meeting prerequisites which are needed by them for effective learning in regular classrooms. Every CwHI is unique as s/he has different needs and requirements. Family background, degree of hearing loss and the age of onset have significant educational implications. Key factors that determine proper inclusion of CwHI include classroom environment, acceptance from teachers and peers, appropriate teaching strategies and use of technology. Therefore, it becomes crucial to make necessary accommodations in classroom settings and strategies that would encourage CwHI to develop academically and socially in regular classrooms.

Classroom Environment

To know CwHI in a classroom is to understand their capabilities and competencies. There are several factors in the classroom that can have an impact on CwHI. It is crucial to identify those factors and work upon them to create suitable environment and strategies for teaching CwHI.

Physical Environment

The very first thing that needs to be assessed is the classroom environment. There should not be cracks in the wall or background noises (traffic outside the class, moving fan, noise of dragging furniture, etc.). All these factors can create obstruction in listening for children who use hearing aids or cochlear implants as it will amplify the unnecessary background noise. However, new digital hearing aids can filter out these noises thereby helping CwHI to listen to the classroom instructions with ease.

Seating Arrangement

1. Visual distractions prevent CwHI from focussing on relevant aspects of classroom and academic tasks. It is therefore necessary to avoid seating CwHI near windows while teaching.
2. The horse-shoe or circular seating arrangement is best suited for CwHI especially those who use sign language as they can see each other while communicating.
3. Place CwHI in front of the classroom so that they do not face difficulty in lip/speech reading.

Classroom Organisation

Classrooms must be organised and teaching-learning materials should be systematically placed. It will help the teacher to focus on students reducing their engagement in disruptive activities.

Movement of a Teacher

Teachers are advised to avoid unnecessary movements in class. Lot of movement in class distracts CwHI and they are not able to pay attention to the oral instructions given by the teacher.

Effects of different degrees of hearing loss on speech, language and probable educational needs

Faintest sound heard	*Effects on understanding language and speech*	*Probable educational needs and programmes*
27 to 40 dB (Slight loss)	• May have difficulty in hearing faint or distant speech • Will usually not have difficulty in school situation	• May benefit from a hearing aid as loss approaches 40dB • Attention to vocabulary development • Needs favourable seating and lighting • May need speech reading instruction • May need speech correction
41 to 55dB (Mild loss)	• Understands conversational speech face to face • May miss as much as 50% of class discussions if voices are faint or not in line of vision • May have limited vocabulary and speech irregularities	• May benefit from individual hearing aid and training in its use • Favourable seating and possible special education supports • Attention to vocabulary and reading is required • May need speech reading instruction
56 to 70 dB (Moderate loss)	• Can understand loud conversation only • Will have increasing difficulty with group discussions • Is likely to have impaired speech • Is likely to have difficulty in language use and comprehension	• Likely to need special/resource teacher or special class • Should have special help in language skills, vocabulary development, usage, reading, writing and grammar etc. • Can benefit from individual hearing and through evaluation, auditory training and speech reading instruction
71 to 90 dB (Severe loss)	• May hear loud voices about 1 foot from the ear • May be able to identify environmental sounds • May be able to discriminate vowels but not all consonants	• Needs specialised programme, supervision and comprehensive support services • Can benefit from individual hearing evaluation • Auditory training on individual and group aids • Part time regular class placement is profitable for student
91 dB or more (Profound loss)	• May hear some loud sounds but sense vibrations more than tonal patterns	• Will need a special education programme for children who are deaf

(*Contd.*)

Faintest sound heard	*Effects on understanding language and speech*	*Probable educational needs and programmes*
	• Relies on vision rather than hearing as primary avenue for communication • Speech and language likely to be impaired	• Needs specialised programme supervision and comprehensive support services • Continuous appraisal of needs in regard to oral or manual communication is required • Auditory training on individual and group aids • Part time regular class placement may be feasible

Source: *W.L. Heward (1996). Exceptional children. In Culatta, R.A. and Tompkins, J.R. (1999).* Fundamentals of special education: What every teacher needs to know. *NJ: Merrill Prentice Hall*

Role of Teacher

It is necessary for teachers to know their teaching subject (content) and subjects (students) whom they teach very well. In an inclusive classroom, each child is unique in her/his abilities and needs. While working with CwHI in a class, one must know about the kind of hearing loss (conductive or sensorineural) and degree of hearing loss (mild, moderate, severe and profound) that they have.

The other important information that teachers must have about CwHI in an inclusive classroom is related to their educational backgrounds. The teacher must know whether the child has previously attended an early intervention centre or a special school or an integral school or is s/he a fresh child who has never been to school and has not received any intervention. Educational background in terms of type of institution attended and enrichment received, and language spoken at home make tremendous difference in interacting with CwHI in inclusive classrooms. All the characteristics of CwHI, as mentioned earlier, play important role in mode of communication used by and for them. Children who can benefit through assistive devices such as hearing aids or other amplification devices can be taught via oral method. Generally, children with severe to profound hearing loss are sign language users. Sign language users are generally people of Deaf community who have strong sense of connect with sign language and consider it as a part of their identity. There are others who use both speech and sign language to communicate.

Teaching Strategies

Certain general points to be adhered to by teachers during classroom transactions are:

- Always face CwHI while teaching them.
- Draw the attention of CwHI before speaking
- Give breaks from listening when necessary. CwHI may fatigue easily because they strain to listen and comprehend
- Keep instructions brief and uncomplicated as much as possible. When repeating instructions, repeat exactly without paraphrasing.
- Restrict unnecessary movements in the classroom
- Provide appropriate classroom environment (acoustic environment) for effective learning
- Avoid wearing stylish dresses, hair styles, ornaments that can distract CwHI while teaching.
- Avoid movement of hands in front of the face while giving oral instructions as it may distract CwHI and hinder their ability to lip/ speech read.
- While teaching, stick to one topic and complete it before moving on to the next one, otherwise CwHI get confused. Context is important for lip readers.

Group Discussion

- Control group discussions so that every student gets a chance to speak. One student speaking at a time works well for learners with hearing impairment; otherwise, it becomes difficult for them to focus if many speakers speak at the same time.
- Encourage whole class discussions and give them the chance to put their views in discussion (verbally or manually).

Teaching-Learning Material

- Ensure that lecture notes and copies of OHTs or PowerPoint slides are available (as a handout or on a website) in advance, if possible, so that CwHI can familiarise themselves with the material and its vocabulary.
- Use visual aids (charts, videos, films, flash cards, models) while teaching to gain their attention. Remember that CwHI grasp content easily if they are provided suitable visual support.

Assignments

- Assess the assignments regularly in order to provide timely feedback and intervention
- Always write the due dates for assignments on the whiteboard/ blackboard.
- While checking assignments, try to focus on the meaning of content written by CwHI than on grammar or vocabulary used. The only exception would be language class where the focus is on language learning.

Other Strategies

- Provide CwHI with a note-taker. The teacher can involve one of the peers to prepare notes of classroom instructions.
- During tests, provide extended time to CwHI.

Role of Peers

Peer interaction plays an important role in child's development and well being. Positive peer interactions and relationships in early childhood play a crucial role on the quality of relationships and social adjustments made in future. In an inclusive set up, CwHI may face difficulties in developing and sustaining positive peer relationships among hearing peers who are used to communicating in a certain manner. Therefore, it is essential to involve hearing peers to facilitate social interaction between them and CwHI.

Following strategies can be employed for supporting interaction between hearing peers and CwHI:

- Provide twenty minute play sessions at least three times per week for small groups of CwHI and hearing peers.
- Orient hearing peers about the needs and abilities of CwHI to support their social integration in the classroom.

Point to Reflect

Rajat is a ten years old boy studying in class V in a regular school. He has moderate hearing loss in both of his ears. He wears BTE (Behind the Ear) hearing aids which attracts every hearing child of his school. Most of his hearings peers make fun of him and pass comments like "dekho yeh hamesha gana sunta rehta hai" while others try to take out his hearing aids. This distresses him and sometimes it becomes the reason for fights between him and his peers.

Why did such a situation arise in the classroom? As a teacher, how will you try to solve this problem in your class?

- If the child with hearing impairment has an fm-system, make sure that it is used on field trips. Ask hearing peers to use microphone and become a tour guide for CwHI.

Peer group plays a crucial role in the psychosocial wellbeing of CwHI. In order to make peer interactions workable and successful, the peer group needs to be sensitised and counselled by the teacher.

Assistive Devices and Technology

All CwHI cannot benefit from assistive listening devices. There is variation in the usage of technologies according to the needs of children, such as the degree of hearing loss and kind of hearing loss. Some of the technologies that can improve the quality of life of CwHI are: Hearing Aids/ FM system, cochlear implants, captioned films/ videos, overhead projectors, laptops and smart boards.

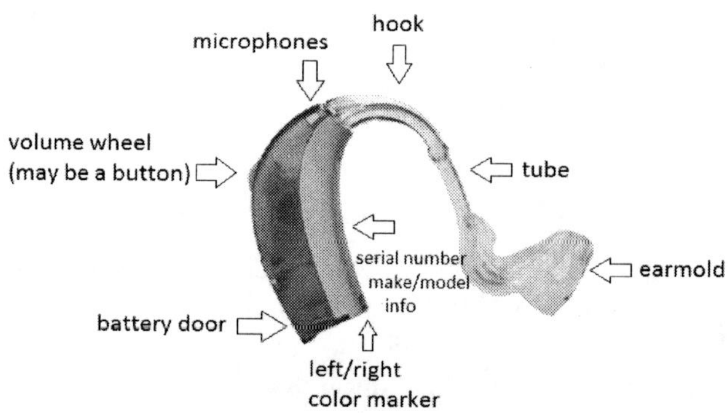

BTE Hearing Aid

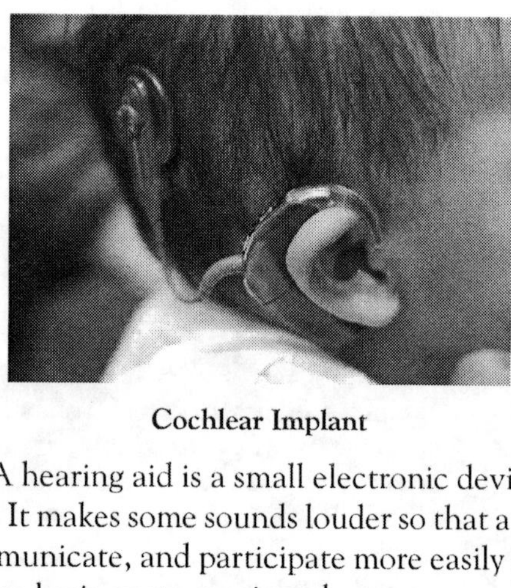

Cochlear Implant

Hearing Aid: A hearing aid is a small electronic device that can be worn in or behind the ear. It makes some sounds louder so that a person with hearing loss can listen, communicate, and participate more easily in daily activities. A hearing aid has three basic parts: a microphone, an amplifier, and a speaker.

The hearing aid receives sound through the microphone, which converts the sound waves into electrical signals and sends them to the amplifier. The amplifier increases the power of the signals and then sends them to the ear through the speaker.

Cochlear Implant: A cochlear implant is a small and complex electronic device that can help to provide a sense of sound to a person who is profoundly deaf or severely hard-of-hearing. The implant consists of an external portion that sits behind the ear and a second portion that is surgically placed under the skin. An implant has the following parts:

- A microphone, which picks up sounds from the environment
- A speech processor, which selects and arranges sounds picked up by the microphone
- A transmitter and a receiver/stimulator, which receive signals from the speech processor and convert them into electric impulses
- An electrode array, which is a group of electrodes that collects the impulses from the stimulator and sends them to different regions of the auditory nerve.

An implant does not restore normal hearing. Instead, it can give a deaf person a useful representation of sounds in the environment and help him/her to understand speech.

FM System: Personal frequency modulation (FM) systems are like miniature radio stations operating on special frequencies. The personal FM system consists of a transmitter microphone used by the speaker (such as the teacher in the classroom, or the speaker at a lecture) and a receiver used by the listener. The receiver transmits the sound to the ears or directly to the hearing aid, in case one is wearing it. It can be used in a variety of places, such as classroom, restaurants, conferences and other larger areas of gathering.

CwHI vary considerably in terms of their degree of hearing loss, age of onset, time of onset whether acquired or congenital and family background. Therefore, every CwHI is unique and has specific needs which can be met only if one has sufficient knowledge about the nature of their hearing loss. These factors have significant educational implications for teaching them. Some children can be benefitted by the use of assistive listening devices while others depend on the use of sign language. The inclusion of CwHI requires a deeper understanding of these children and their individual needs. It is thus essential for teachers to know the children's language needs, their family backgrounds and the nature of deafness so that appropriate teaching strategies can be developed. The chapter focuses on CwHI who can be educated in aural/oral environment where students are taught through verbal mode. The following diagram, in a nutshell, provides suggestions for effective education of CwHI in an inclusive setting:

Suggestions for the Classroom

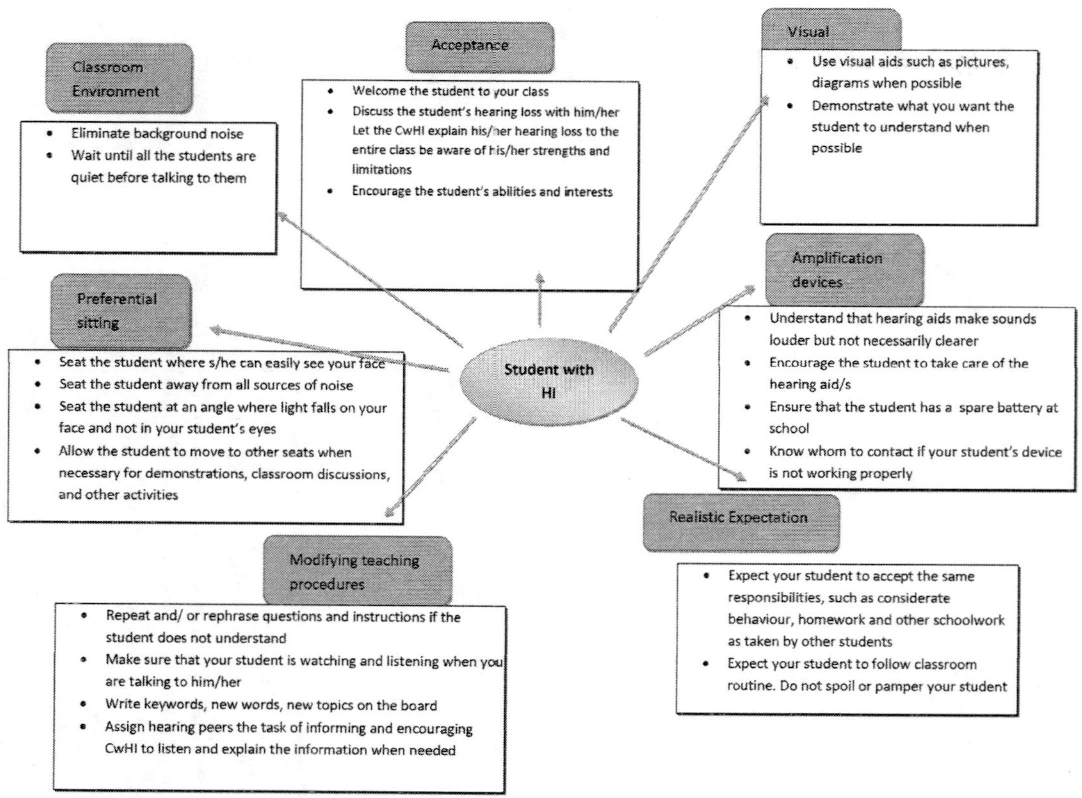

Conclusion

There is significant diversity among the group of persons with hearing impairment: some may hear too little, others better and still others may not be able to hear at all. Thus the communication needs of children with hearing impairment would correspond to various approaches of communication. It includes aural/oral approach which supports speech as a mode of communication and manual approach that encourages the use of sign language, gestures, finger spelling and cued speech. The behavioural manifestations of children with hearing impairment are very important for a teacher to know to identify them in their classrooms and to help in their formal screening and assessment.

The key components that determine the effective inclusion of children with hearing impairments are classroom environment, role of teachers, teaching strategies, teaching learning material, role of peers and the assistive devices.

REFERENCES

Gargiulo, R.M. (2015). *Special Education in Contemporary Society: An Introduction to Exceptionality*, Los Angeles: SAGE Publications.

Gathoo, V. (2016, March). I have a deaf child in my class, what do I need to know? Symposium on Disability, Mental Health, and Teacher Preparation conducted at University of Delhi, Delhi.

Gudyanga, E., Wadesango, N., Eliphanos Hove, Gudyanga, A. and Mediterranean (2014). "Challenges Faced by Students with Hearing Impairment in Bulawayo Urban Regular Schools", *Journal of Social Sciences*., 5(9).

Kemple, K.M. (2014). *Let's be Friends: Peer Competence and Social Inclusion in Early Childhood Programmes*. New York. Teachers College Press.

Knoors, H. and Marschark, M. (2012). Language planning for the 21st century: Revisiting bilingual language policy for deaf children. *Journal of Deaf Studies and Deaf Education, 17: 291-305.*

Kunnen, E.S. (2014). "Identity development in deaf adolescents", *Journal of Deaf Studies and Deaf Education. 1-12.*

Mangal, S.K. (2007). *Educating exceptional children: An Introduction to Special Education*, PHI Learning Private Limited.

Norman, P., Chandran, M. and Dhandapani, T. (2016). "Prevalence of Hearing Impairment in School Children (Aged 8-14 Years) in the Villages of Vadamavanthal", Tamil Nadu, India. *International Journal of Community Medicine and Public Health*, 3(12).

Nunes, T., Pretzlik, U. and Olsson, J. (2001). "Deaf Children's Social Relationships in Mainstream Schools". *Deafness and Education International*, 3(3): 123-136.

Smith, T.E., Polloway, E.A., Doughty, T.T., Patton, J.R. and Dowdy, C.A. (2013). *Teaching students with Special Needs in Inclusive Settings*. Delhi: PHI Learning Private Limited.

W.L. Heward (1996). "Exceptional Children", In: Culatta, R.A. and Tompkins, J.R. (1999). *Fundamentals of special education: What every teacher needs to know*. NJ: Merill Prentice Hall

Web Resources

Structure of ear (n.d.). Retrieved from http://simplebiologyy.blogspot.in/2014/11/human-ear-outer-ear-middle-ear-inner-ear-hearing.html
http://www.aiishmysore.in/en/pdf/pe_pamphlets/child_hearing.pdf
http://www.handsandvoices.org/needs/socialization.htm
http://www.rehabcouncil.nic.in/writereaddata/hi.pdf
http://www.who.int/mediacentre/factsheets/fs300/en/
https://www.asha.org
https://www.nidcd.nih.gov
http://wordinfo.info/unit/620/ip:1/il:D

4

Intellectual Disability and Inclusionary Practice

The Way Forward

Kavita Ghosh

Intellectual Disability (ID) is a form of disability characterised by sub-average mental functioning of an individual; it is a condition that arises due to improper growth of the brain and the nervous system. Intellectual impairment is caused as the rate of growth and development of one's intellectual powers gets diminished or arrested (Mangal, 2007).

ID can be of varying degrees starting from mild to moderate to severe and profound. ID is a high incidence disability. Indian Council of Medical Research states that 12.8 per cent of children have mental and behavioural disorders. While working with children with ID, it becomes imperative that one should have a complete understanding of their strengths and limitations and know how to create an emotionally safe and conducive environment for them to develop in a healthy manner. ID should not be merely looked at as a condition of the brain and the nervous system, rather there is a need to look at ID in the wider socio-cultural milieu. Similarly, persons with intellectual disability (PWID) should essentially be seen as human beings first rather than as medical cases with special brain conditions. The premise in this chapter is that with certain modifications in the curriculum and an understanding of the specific learning and socio-emotional needs of children suffering from mild and moderate ID, a teacher can accommodate such learners in the regular class with the support of other school staff, parents and community at large.

Nurturing and working with a person with intellectual disability is a great learning and transformational experience. It is a rare opportunity to have insights into the functioning of human mind and its inner growth. Any attempt to bring change can be successful only when we shift from self-centric approach to person-centric view. We must value, understand and appreciate the persons with intellectual disability completely. We need to accept less than perfect ways of doing and being, develop patience and perseverance, nurture more respect for such people. Growth opportunities need to be available in the form of appropriate education, work, friendships, recreational facilities and support services for families.

The paper primarily focuses on the functional aspects of identifying and including the learners with mild and moderate level of ID in the regular classroom which most of the times is not given any serious consideration. The term 'mild' is particularly looked at as insignificant in terms of giving special care to children with mild or moderate ID. It needs to be emphasised that to identify the needs of severely intellectually disabled children and to provide them with special care falls into the ambit of special schools and there is a need to understand their significance in terms of catering to individuals with severe and profound levels of disabilities.

In the context of their education, it is important to understand that there could also be learners in class who are affected by other forms of disabilities, such as specific learning disability or loco-motor, hearing and visually impairment. Considering the class as a unit and there being the possibility of having learners with varied academic and socio-emotional needs, the task of the teacher becomes very demanding and this calls for meticulous planning. This chapter gives some insights about ID and the overall social and educational support that can be given to PWID for them to flourish as part of the larger society.

Two most crucial aspects to understand intellectual disability are intellectual functioning and adaptive behaviour, as mentioned in 'The Rights of Persons with Disability Act' (PWD Act), 2016.

I. Intellectual functioning, also called intelligence, refers to a general mental capacity such as learning, reasoning, problem-solving and so on. It is measured through IQ tests. Generally, an IQ score of 70-75 indicates a limitation in intellectual functioning.

II. Adaptive behaviour is the collection of conceptual, social and practical skills that are learned and performed by people in their everyday lives.

(i) Conceptual skills include language and literacy, money, time and number concepts, and self-direction.

(ii) Social skills include interpersonal skills, sense of social responsibility, self-esteem, social problem-solving skills and the ability to follow rules and laws, and avoid getting victimised.

(iii) Practical skills refer to activities of daily living which include eating, mobility, using toilets and dressing, occupational skills, health care, taking medication, travel safety, telephone use, housekeeping, etc.

It is important to understand the kind of cognitive functions that get affected in Persons with Intellectual Disability (PWID), the problems this poses for them and the kind of support required to enable them to develop their maximum potential. Our cognitive ability helps us to understand the world around us. As there is inadequate development of brain and nervous system in PWID, their day-to-day learning and social adjustments are not at par with their chronological age. Cognitive processes such as attention, perception, memory, concept formation, thinking and reasoning, planning and problem-solving that affect the scope for learning are not properly developed in the PWID. Moreover, all of these processes are inter-linked, and thus improper development of one affects the other processes as well. PWID better adapt at learning through concrete objects and sensory exposures. However, their ability to think in abstract terms is restricted. It is important to understand that majority of learning in schools is around abstract thinking and metacognition, and thus is not appropriate for PWID. For them, learning experiences that are centered on concrete experiences and are carried out in a routine structured manner with little change are more fruitful. Equally important it is to give them an emotionally safe and sound environment where they are trusted and treated with respect. Continuous and consistent efforts are to be made to help the PWID develop a sense of self.

Intellectual disability is a disability characterised by significant limitations in both intellectual functioning and adaptive behaviour. Several definitions have been proposed and numerous terminologies have been used to denote intellectual impairment, the most common being, 'mentally retarded', 'mentally handicapped', 'mentally challenged', 'general learning disability' and so on. However, there has been a shift from the deficiency model to the support model. Since 2008, professionally, the term 'Intellectual Disability' is being used more often. In 2008, the American Association on Intellectual and Developmental Disabilities (AAIDD) recommended the use of the term 'Intellectual Disability' in place of 'Mental Retardation'.

It is now being widely understood that intellectual disability:

- Is not merely about a deficit within an individual; it is also about the environment and the kinds and levels of support needed by the individual to function effectively.
- Is not an inherent trait or permanent state of being. Rather, it emphasises that a degree of one's intellectual impairment is reflected through one's present functioning and the environmental support is needed to improve it.

- Focuses more on the needs of the individual instead of degrees of deficiency within the affected individuals.
- Is not about only sub-average intellectual functioning, but may also be about limitations in performance and adaptive skills.
- Should not be treated as the distinguishing factor between PWID and other people. They are more similar than different in terms of their emotional and social needs.
- Manifests during the developmental period, i.e. within 18 years of age.

Causes of Intellectual Disability

Intellectual disability is caused when the brain gets injured or a problem prevents the brain from developing normally. These problems can happen while the baby is growing inside the womb, during birth, or after the baby is born. Many a times, even doctors do not know the cause.

Following are some problems that can cause intellectual disabilities:

- Problems in the baby's genes, which are in every cell of the baby and determine how the body will develop, can cause ID. (Genes are inherited from both parents and the baby might receive genes that are abnormal or genes might change while the baby is developing.)
- Problems during pregnancy can cause ID. Sometimes, the mother might contract an infection or illness that can harm the baby. Certain medicines used by the mother during pregnancy can cause problems for the baby. Consumption of alcohol or illegal drugs also can damage a baby's developing brain.
- Insufficient supply of oxygen during childbirth.
- Premature birth.
- Serious brain infection soon after birth.
- A serious head injury can hurt the brain and cause intellectual disabilities at any point in life. Some of these disabilities are temporary and others can be permanent. (This explains the need to wear a helmet while riding a bike and a seatbelt while driving a car!)

Manifestation and Identification of Mild and Moderate Intellectual Disability

Generally, the score on an intelligence test is taken as an important indicator of any possible intellectual impairment. The score and the observation records of the adaptive skills of the individuals are used to decide the severity of ID.

Here, it is important to understand that depending upon the support and encouragement provided during learning, understanding of the psychological and emotional needs of the person and the nurturing and caring environment provided, and PWID's chances of performing to the best of their abilities are heightened. While categorisation of PWID into mild or moderate may help to an extent, more important is the physical, social and emotional environment that is provided to them. Thus, it is important to appreciate them more for what they have and what they can do.

In order to identify a child with intellectual impairment, following measures need to be considered carefully:

- Identification must be carried out within the developmental period, i.e. within 18 years of age.
- Behaviour should be well observed for detecting deficiencies in adaptive behaviour.
- In case the adaptive behaviour indicates possible intellectual impairment, it should be confirmed through intelligence test or vice-versa.
- A low IQ and deficient adaptive behaviour, both should be used as criteria for detecting intellectual impairment.
- The judgement regarding one's intellectual impairment must be made after taking into consideration the existing environmental conditions.

Depending upon the level of severity, the PWID are categorised in four groups: mild, moderate, severe and profound. Different levels of ID manifest differently in day-to-day functioning and behaviour. Following are some typical manifestations of mild and moderate levels of ID.

A. *Mild Intellectual Disability*

Individuals with mild intellectual impairment demonstrate adaptive behaviour and intellectual functioning at the upper end of the retardation continuum. According to AAMR (Grossman, 1983) definition, assessed intellectual functioning of individuals with mild retardation is within the IQ range of 50-55 to approximately 70 points, with concurrent deficit in adaptive behaviour (Thomas & Patton, 1990, p. 198).

In terms of behavioural characteristics, some of the specific problem areas include disruptiveness, attention deficit, low self-esteem, over activity, distractibility and other attention related problems. Due to lack of comparable verbal and communication skills, they may withdraw from interpersonal relationships. They generally cannot distinguish between acceptable and non–

acceptable standards of behaviour. Problem behaviour can also result from frustration caused be scholastic failure and a strong desire to win the approval of their peers. They may be identified as slow learners and speech disturbances are common among them. In comparison to people in general, the individuals with ID find it difficult to control their impulses and also take time to understand the consequences of their actions.

The cause of ID in most cases of mild intellectual impairment is unknown. While hereditary factors are an etiological consideration at any level, other variables such as nutrition, health care and environmental stimulation play important roles as well. While the slower rate at which these children develop motor, social and language skills may be noticeably different from their peers, mild intellectual disability is often suspected when children entre school. Often a combination of difficulties with academic subjects and behavioural problems generate concern (Thomas & Patton, 1990, p. 198-199). Majority or approximately 85 per cent of cases of ID are only mild in intensity.

B. Moderate Intellectual Disability

Chances are that children who function below a mild level of intellectual impairment are identified earlier than children with mild ID. Children with moderate ID are usually identified prior to school entry. Very young children who have moderate intellectual impairment will demonstrate developmental delays in skills such as sitting, crawling, walking and especially language acquisition. Children with moderate intellectual impairment are those who display significant deficits in adaptive behaviour and function intellectually within the 30-35 IQ range. Approximately 10 per cent of the total ID population has moderate level of ID.

Individuals with moderate intellectual disability would exhibit more behavioural disorders than those with mild intellectual disability. A wide range of behaviours may be demonstrated by such individuals including distractibility, hyperactivity, mood disturbances and stereotypical behaviours. Health related problems as well as medication may impact attention and concentration leading to a slower and more limited acquisition of social skills and to an increase in inappropriate behaviours. The difficulty in acquiring motor and language skills as well as physical and health problems make the case visible for special assistance and guidance.

Children with moderate intellectual impairment may have multiple disabling conditions. Various clinical syndromes, notably, Down Syndrome, are often associated with moderate intellectual impairment which produces distinct physical characteristics (Thomas & Patton, 1990, p. 203). However, there is a wide variation in mental abilities and developmental progress in children with Down syndrome. Not all children affected by Down syndrome have ID. Though it is observed that the majority of children with Down syndrome function in the mild to moderate range of mental retardation, some children are not mentally retarded at all. They may function in the borderline to low average range; others may be severely mentally retarded. (*Source:* http://www.ds-health.com/pueschel.htm).

General Symptoms: Overall, certain general symptoms in children with ID include:

- Delay in sitting, standing, walking or talking
- Difficulty in learning everyday skills, such as eating, dressing, combing, toilet cleaning, tying shoe laces, cutting with scissors, holding a pencil and so on
- Difficulty in following instructions and expressing oneself
- Low attention span and memory
- Aggression, anxiety and withdrawal exhibited through behaviour
- Fits or occasional loss of consciousness.

Categories of mild, moderate, severe and profound levels of intellectual disability are defined on the basis of IQ scores. Some students will require greater support than others will.

Mild Intellectual Disability

A mild intellectual disability is defined as an IQ between 50 and 70.

- Can participate independently in most leisure activities within their communities
- Will have important relationships with the people in their lives
- May marry and raise a family with support
- May have a job suited to their skills, struggle in certain social situations
- May live and travel independently with support
- May need help to handle money and to plan and organise their daily routine
- May learn to read and write in appropriate educational setting
- Likely to develop reading, writing, and math skills at a basic level.

Moderate Intellectual Disability

A moderate intellectual disability is defined as an IQ between 35 and 50.

- Will have important relationships with the people in their lives

- May learn to navigate within their community and travel with support
- Will have difficulty planning trips and handling money independently
- Will recognise environmental print (e.g. signs, logos, sight words) in daily life
- Will need visual prompts, such as daily schedules and pictures of routines
- Will need support in their daily lives
- May display independence in certain daily activities, such as dressing and bathing.

Severe or Profound Intellectual Disability

A severe intellectual disability is defined as an IQ between 20 and 35. A profound intellectual disability is defined as an IQ below 20.

- May have little or no speech and will rely on gestures, facial expressions, and body language to communicate needs or feelings
- Will require functional communication systems (e.g. low or high tech augmentative communication devices) in order to express their wants and needs
- Will need visual prompts, such as daily schedules and pictures of routines
- Will require extensive support with daily living activities throughout their lives

Source: do2learn.com/disabilities/CharacteristicsAndStrategies/IntellectualDisability_Characteristics.html

Misconceptions about Intellectual Disability

There are certain misconceptions about ID and people affected by it. We all need to be cautious of the fact that though some individuals have ID but first and foremost they are human beings. Labeling gives rise to increased differentiation and prejudice. Nature exhibits diversity in various forms. Human beings differ greatly from each other in numerous ways, namely inclinations, interests, dispositions, beliefs, etc. We need to acknowledge this diversity and accept it. Due to lack of knowledge, there are numerous misconceptions that are harbored and propagated in the society. There is a strong need to generate awareness about ID to ensure just and sensitive treatment of PWID by other members of the society.

Myths and Facts about ID

Myth	*Fact*
Intellectual disability is a hereditary problem.	Intellectual disability is only sometimes inherited. Most often, it is caused by external influences, some of which can be prevented.
Intellectual disability is contagious.	Intellectual disability does not spread by any type of contact.
Children with intellectual disability can never be disciplined.	Like all children, children with intellectual disability also need to be taught good behaviour. However, it is important to take their limitations into consideration while disciplining them.
Marriage can cure intellectual disability.	Marriage to a person with intellectual disability must take place with the full consent of the partner, who should be informed about the medical condition of the person.
Medicines and vitamins can cure intellectual disability.	When intellectual disability is caused by a treatable condition, appropriate treatment of that condition can cure it. There are, however, no tonics that can totally cure the impaired brain functions.
Students with intellectual disabilities cannot learn to read.	Many students with intellectual disabilities are able to learn to read. It may take specific interventions, or different pathways, and longer than usual, but reading skills are attainable.
Students with intellectual disabilities cannot be successful in the general education setting.	Not only can students with ID make academic gains within the general education setting, there is evidence that social skills development is better supported while being educated alongside non-disabled peers.

Source: http://www.whiteswanfoundation.org/article/intellectual-disability-mental-retardation-myths-and-facts/ https://www.kennedykrieger.org/professional-training/training-disciplines/special-education-fellowship/linking-research-classrooms-blog/myths-facts-intellectual-disabilities).

Academic and Psycho-Social Adaptations by the Teacher

From the first day of school, children depend on their teachers to provide them with the understanding and support that allows them to get the most out of their daily interactions in the classroom. Positive relationships with teachers serve as a secure base for young students. In an inclusive school, teachers are encouraged to develop reflective practices and adapt current pedagogical practices, knowledge so as to apply them in different ways to create

The United Nations Conventions on the Rights of People with Disabilities (UNCRPD) is a path breaking step in recognising the human rights of people with disabilities and bringing a paradigm shift from a welfare approach to a right-based approach. India ratified this international legislation in 2007. It means that the Government of India has a commitment to enable people with all disabilities to exercise their human rights.

Source: http://www.muskaanthengo.org/what-muskaan-do/awareness-advocac y/

an inclusive classroom. Teaching and assessment practices are aligned so that each is in cognizance with the other. Teachers focus on creating learning experiences that are positive, success-oriented, and foster learning through reasonable learning activities. In an inclusive school, even the school management recognises that teachers may require additional support in developing and using teaching and learning strategies that facilitate the inclusion of pupils with special educational needs.

The truth, however, is that a significant proportion of children with disabilities are denied access to basic services including education and healthcare (https://www.unicef.org/disabilities/files/Factsheet_A5_Web_NEW.pdf). These services play a crucial role in early diagnosis and early intervention which further help in treating the condition in a better way and reduce the chances of further complication (Mangal, 2007).

Polloway *et al.* (2010). highlight the relative absence of recent research on educational intervention for mildly or moderately intellectually disabled. Placement of ID children continues to take place in special classes or separate classes outside the purview of general education. However, the adaptations suggested here should be seen in the context of including children with mild and moderate ID in regular classrooms. While persons with mild intellectual disabilities have been described as members of a "forgotten generation" (Tymchuk *et al.*, 2001), they warrant the continued attention of educators. An emphasis on research related to this population and further development of validated, successful educational practices remains paramount (p. 67).

Students with mild and moderate intellectual disability can in many cases be educated within the regular classroom by using materials and methods

The RTE Act attempts to provide an enabling environment for disabled children to enter school, attend and complete elementary education. The Right of Children to Free and Compulsory Education Act, 2009 states "Provided that a child suffering from disability in clause (i) of Section 2 of 'the Persons with Disabilities (Equal Opportunities, Protection and Full Participation) Act 1996', shall have the right to pursue free and compulsory elementary education in accordance with the provisions of chapter V of the above said act". (Chapter 2, Section 2) proven to be effective for students with special needs. A few areas need a mention in this regard namely suitable placement of children with ID, modification of content and teaching-learning strategies, and the use of advanced technology for their benefit.

Placement Considerations

Depending upon the level of ID, following placement alternatives for children with ID may be considered in the context of a developing country such as ours.

- Regular schools
- Regular schools with the provision of a resource room
- Regular schools with the provision of special classes
- Special schools
- Residential special schools
- Home and hospital bound educational facilities.

Enrolling children with mild and moderate ID in regular schools without proper modification of curriculum could be detrimental to their growth. The second alternative of 'regular schools with the provision of a resource room' may work well for children with mild and moderate ID. These children, at the school level, may be assigned to resource sections of the academic subjects. They can be taught both by special educators on some occasions and regular teachers along with other children on others. Regular schools with the provision of special classes can only be practical in case there is good number of mild and moderate ID children. All the provisions and facilities needed by children with mild and moderate ID should be made available through these special classes. The last three placement options are required in the cases of severe and profound level of IDs.

Curriculum Adaptations and Instructional Methodology

Teachers of PWID tend to struggle and face challenges. They require inner transformation in terms of attitudes and values. They should be able to understand and manage the developmental levels and needs of each student of the class. The teachers must try to design appropriate goals, programme(s), and assessment for each student. They should be able to maintain high level of motivation and efforts despite very slow process of change and development shown by their students. They need to deal with effects of teacher burnt-out and build up inner resources for continued efforts.

The curriculum for children with ID should be designed in a way that ensures their maximum participation and learning both conceptually and in terms of social skills. While in the case of disabilities such as visual, loco-motor, hearing and others, the National Focus Group on 'Education of children with special needs' (NCERT, 2006) emphasises the need of same curriculum, in case of children with ID, it too mentions the need of special curriculum keeping into consideration their cognitive and behavioural concerns.

Looking from the perspective of developmental stages given by Piaget in his Cognitive-developmental theory, there are certain important observations made by Inhelder (1968) and Woodward (1963, 1979). According to them, a child with intellectual impairment progressed through the same stages of intellectual development as the child with average intellectual capacity, with the major differences being in the rate and highest levels achieved. Intellectually disabled children may not be able to reach all the stages of development. According to Inhelder, children who are mildly intellectual impaired may reach the concrete operational level but individuals who are moderately intellectual impaired will go no further than the sensorimotor stage. Teachers of children with ID need to be aware of the developmental sequence in order to determine a child's readiness for a particular task and to consider the slow rate and the expected optimum level of functioning when planning curricula for varying levels of intellectual impairment (Patton, Pyne & Smith, 1990, pp. 209-210).

Curriculum planning involves variation of curricular content, processes and products. Curriculum planning aims at maximising pupil involvement while maintaining the integrity of the subject matter and providing meaningful access to a wide, rich and age-appropriate curriculum. Curricular planning is done in a manner to promote pupil participation, and provide a sense of accomplishment to all the learners.

Content related adaptations for children with mild and moderate ID revolve around four skill areas as follows (Mangal, 2007):

- Development of basic reading and arithmetic skills: These skills are significant to carry out simple day-to-day tasks that are expected from children with mild and moderate ID.
- Development of language and communication skills: Basic language and communication skills are important as they provide the medium to the child to communicate his/her needs and emotions to others and understand them as well. Language is the medium to learn further important concepts.
- Development of social skills: This set of skills refers to self-care and a sense of family and community living. Acquiring and cultivating social skills help children to learn from their peers and engage in group activities, such as interacting with people, playing games and so on.

- Development of vocational skills: This includes encouraging the child to develop habits of following simple instructions, paying attention, persistence and group co-operation. Children can gradually be involved in arts and craft activities and in the use of simple machines and apparatus to assist them to choose some vocation.
- Other areas of development such as sensory, physical and emotional also need to be dealt with care. Quite important is the area of emotional health as it is related to one's overall well-being. People with ID are often commented upon and are subject to ridicule. What they need is love and respect in order to function appropriately.

Daily activities and learning experiences should help the children with ID to strengthen their cognitive processes such as attention, perception, memory, concept formation, thinking and reasoning, planning and problem-solving so that they have better chances of learning. Almost all the activities of everyday life require cognitive functions. This is true for everyone including persons with intellectual disability. It is important to note that one does not need to do any special activities to build cognition. Normal everyday activities, such as bathing, eating food, going for an outing, everyday conversation and interaction are the best opportunities to enrich a child with information. Recognising and naming common utility items, awareness about one's needs and feelings as well as of others, following instructions, understanding others' expectations, understanding do's and don'ts and the reasons of it, familiarity with social environment are various activities which constantly use our cognitive capabilities. It is important to remember that conversation must go on along with these activities to facilitate comprehension.

The most important thing is to provide input on a regular basis. Any teaching done inconsistently or irregularly is not likely to yield desired results. The sooner such activities start, the easier it is for learning to take place.

Enhancing cognitive functioning means strengthening cognitive functions mentioned in the previous series. Almost every activity requires these functions as discussed below.

Attention: Any activity that engages one for some period of time enhances the attention power. It could be a game, sports activity, listening to music, watching TV, carrying on one's assigned task e.g., arranging one's belongings, laying table for meals, watering plants or filling water bottles, etc.

Sensory functioning involving vision, hearing, touch, taste and smell: Recognition of objects and people through seeing, hearing or picture recognition enhances the power to construct images in one's mind. Watching TV can be a rich source of building imagery, vocabulary, recognition of emotions and social situations.

Memory: Memory reflects itself in recall, recognition and reproduction. Reinforcing recognition and recall in everyday interaction would strengthen memory.

Concept development: A concept is the set of rules used to define the categories of objects, things, events, people, and emotions and so on. They help us to make sense of our physical and social environment. The more the number of concepts one has, the greater the understanding one possesses of things around. Concepts can range from concrete (clothes, vegetables, various utility items etc.) to abstract (time, numbers, space etc.). Most learning is based on concepts. The steps involved in the process of concept formation are: Observing and identifying similarities and differences, Matching (identifying and putting together things which are identical), Classifying (putting together things that have some characteristic in common), Comparing and seriating (Comparing involves establishing a relation between two objects based on some specific characteristic, such as size, texture, shade, etc. Seriation or gradation refers to arranging objects in a graded fashion either in increasing or decreasing order based on some specific characteristic.

Thinking and Reasoning: Putting together concepts according to certain rules that convey meaningful information involves thinking and reasoning. Uttering a simple sentence 'I am thirsty' reflects the thought behind it. People with intellectual disability have serious difficulty in abstract thinking but not so much in concrete thinking because it connects to observable things and situations.

Patience, perseverance, consistent effort, encouraging attitude, positive outlook and recognition of the learning difficulties of children are of utmost importance for anyone working with children with ID. One has to shift from self-centric to person-centric approach, i.e., focus on the difficulties of the person rather than one's own frustrations, disappointments and difficulties. Such an approach is bound to bring about positive results in learning, capacity building and emotional well-being of the challenged person.

Curricular Guidelines: Understanding of certain overall guidelines will go a long way in bringing out the best in PWID in general and children with mild and moderate ID in particular.

- *Progressing from simple to complex:* Simple concepts should be introduced before coming to relatively more difficult concepts. There should be an active interaction with the physical and the social world coupled with repeated explanations and encouragement through positive feedback so that concepts are learnt effectively. Though language plays an important role, it is not a big limiting factor. Most of the people with intellectual disability have fairly good receptive language, though they may be non-verbal. Use of pictures and gestures will also be beneficial.

- *Progressing from concrete to abstract:* High and complex level of abstraction should not be expected from ID children. Concrete materials should always be used for a considerable time period before moving to even simplest level of abstraction. Explanations should be simple, both at the level of language used and meaning. Teachers need to present stimuli that vary in only a few dimensions and draw students' attention towards these dimensions.
- *Progressing from whole two parts:* Unnecessary and trivial breaking down of concepts into smaller chunks should be avoided. Teachers should provide a holistic experience before bringing attention to its parts. To facilitate recall, teachers must organise the material into meaningful segments and give verbal prompts. Repetition and drill helps children with ID in retention of the concepts.
- If parents and teachers make it a habit to explain things including what, why, where, when and how in our explanation, children with ID can develop elementary reasoning or logical thinking.
- *Encouraging multi-sensory learning:* Involvement of all the senses will not only engage the learner in the learning process but will also help in retention of concepts learnt.
- *Encouraging learning by doing:* Instead of making learning dull and alien, they should learn while doing and performing educationally designed tasks. Instructions and information should be presented in small and sequential steps. It should be reviewed frequently.
- *Providing encouragement and positive feedback:* In order to help them sustain their efforts in learning, children with ID must always be encouraged and acknowledged for their efforts. It boosts their self-image, confidence and initiative for learning.
- *Peer tutoring:* Children with mild ID, when placed with average children, learn a lot from them by imitating their behaviour.
- Behaviour management technique: With the help of a special educator, following techniques can be implemented. (Also elaborated in the section: 'working with special educators').
    a. *Differentiated Reinforcement:* Whenever desired behaviour is displayed, positive reinforcement should be provided in the form of eatables, verbal and non-verbal praise, etc.
    b. Observational learning such as modeling can be effectively used with all children but it has specific mportance for children with ID due to their outer directed tendency. Teachers should be aware that their behaviour is being watched and can be imitated. They

need to model desirable behaviour and should draw attention towards students exhibiting desirable behaviour. Ignoring undesirable behaviour is also important. Audio-visual and live models can be introduced.

c. Assisting, cueing and prompting can help children at different stages of work assignment.
d. *Token System:* A small token-like item can be provided for display of desired behaviour and the same can be withheld in case of some undesirable behaviour. Later these tokens can be exchanged periodically for something enjoyable for the child.

A. Constructive Use of Technological Advancements

Children with ID face a lot of difficulties in acquiring basic skills related to day-to-day living. Simple software could be used to help those drill and practice skills with the help of recorded voice, visuals and proper sequencing.

Collaboration between Professionals and the Role of Parents

Polloway *et al.* (2010) quote Hoover & Patton (2005, 2008): "Any trend toward inclusion is inescapably linked to how well the general education setting is prepared to handle students who will require differentiated strategies in terms of content, instructional materials, instruction, assignments, testing, products, setting and management. Collaborative arrangement with special educator and other school staff is needed. So, it becomes a multi-tiered system with tier 1 involving preventive efforts (enhanced instruction in general education) and tier 2 involving supportive efforts (ongoing collaboration in general education)" (p. 61).

Including children with mild and moderate ID is not possible if the teacher does not get enough and timely support from other stakeholders. The role of special educator is thus very important in providing the right guidance to the teachers who work with children with ID.

Children with, or at risk for, developmental disabilities must be identified and served as early as possible. Parents can play a pivotal role in the diagnosis of ID in children, and thus make early intervention possible. Measurable, cost-effective and sound intervention will advance the development of children and support their health. Families are the constant and the primary source of life-long support and early learning in children's lives. Families should be supported in making informed decisions and in partnering effectively with professionals to achieve positive outcomes.

To bring large number of special children in the classroom, there is a need to introduce major changes in our school infrastructure and teacher training curriculum. A counsellor would also be required. Special educators, with the help of class teachers and parents, can opt for the following therapies in order to help children with mild and moderate ID to adjust better socially and emotionally:

- *Individual Counselling:* Children with mild ID can particularly benefit from counselling as they can understand and respond in a conversation. Being heard is psychologically comforting for them.
- *Cognitive therapy:* This therapy is better suited for children with mild ID. In this, the educator tries to talk to the child and makes him/her think of the situation when he/she feels troubled and helps him/her to think of alternatives.
- *Family therapy:* This is indeed required for the families with children suffering from any level of ID. The basic idea is to help the family members to extend their support and help the child become as independent as possible. Both educational and emotional support from family members is discussed and encouraged.
- *Activity therapy:* It is an innovative therapy in which constructive media such as music, art, sports and so on are used to channelise the child's energy. Attempt is made to build self-confidence, positive self-concept and positive life experiences in children with ID.
- *Peer Tutoring:* Other able learners in the class can be paired up with learners with ID. They will not only act as role models for them but also assist them in tasks as guided by the teacher. It is helpful for both disabled and other able learners, as the learner with ID gets the needed assistance and other learners develop a healthy and positive attitude for their friends with ID.
- *Behaviour Management:* Through this approach, a consistent and structural framework is adopted to teach appropriate behaviour in order to replace the maladaptive behaviour in children with ID. It is expected that both at school and at home, the behavioural needs of the child are looked at in the same way and the same therapy(s) should be followed to avoid contradiction.

Parents of PWID deal with the loss of self-image and consequent grief and frustration. For them, it is a long struggle with oneself. They lack proper understanding about intellectual disability and its impact on the person. They need to build up psychological and physical resources and manage demands of time, energy and patience. The parents often struggle due to lack of needed support services.

The persons with intellectual disability encounter immense challenges. Some of these challenges include inadequate conceptual learning, which creates confusion in comprehending the demands of living and environment. Furthermore, repeated experiences of failure kill the initiative for learning and build up a resistance towards learning. Unsympathetic attitudes of parents and others, and lack of positive experiences deal severe blows to their self-image causing several emotional and behavioural difficulties. They have to deal with serious deprivations and inappropriate treatment. Majority of them have no access to education, training, employment and other opportunities that help us in living a life of dignity. They try hard to cope with a world that does not function as per their needs and their personhood is not recognised. They are denied the mundane pleasures of life and constantly rely on other people for survival. There is a lot of social stigma, isolation, neglect and ridicule that they have to face, in addition to the lack of learning opportunities, schooling and productive work.

There are many barriers to the growth, development and fuller life of the persons with intellectual disability. These are due to the lack of appropriate interventions, education, training and work opportunities, impoverished social learning environment, poor understanding of their psychological needs including social and emotional needs by their care givers, near zero expectations from them in every domain. The attitudes towards ID get manifested explicitly in their non-acceptance, neglect and marginalisation by the mainstream. The utilitarian notions of larger society including family, grossly undermines their worth.

PWID are talked about or criticised by people around them, often in front of them. Sometimes their parents get so overwhelmed by their own hardships that they forget to notice theirs. Their problems are compounded by the fact that neither can they share them with others nor do they know how to deal with them. Stubborn, disruptive and aggressive behaviour is always a manifestation of their frustrations, anger and hurt. They experience many more failures and neglect than other people. Therefore, they need extra care of their physical, cognitive and emotional needs. Total acceptance of their condition and unconditional love is the first step towards emotional care. Emotional well-being is crucial for effective functioning of children and adults with intellectual disability. We can take care of their emotional well-being by keeping in mind the Dos and Don'ts mentioned in the following box.

Dos and Don'ts

- Talk to them as often as you can about routine things, e.g., what breakfast to eat, dishes for lunch or dinner, outings, about people coming over, preference for music and other such things.

- Involve them frequently in conversations with others.
- When they become stubborn, give them a hug and ask what is troubling them and how it creates difficulty for everyone in the family.
- Give frequent hugs to express love and care.
- In quiet moments, tell them how their undesirable conduct is hurting you, also because others will not think well of them.
- Appreciate their achievement, even if it is a small one.
- Make them feel valued and respected for whatever they are. It will happen automatically if you genuinely value them as a person. Treat them as a person with their own pleasures and pains. This demands certain level of objectivity and maturity. Others will respect them depending upon how much love and respect they receive at home.
- Never criticise them in front of others. If they need to be told to behave properly, take them aside and explain the situation.
- Stop thinking "if he/she was normal"; it will cause hindrance towards their unconditional acceptance. This will also cause more pain and frustration which is futile.
- Avoid being harsh with them. If it does happen, do apologise for it.
- Do not ignore undesirable expression of emotions. Deal with it firmly and clearly, always followed by explanations.

Persons with Intellectual disability function better within a structured environment. They feel more comfortable in working within a routine without much change in it. Helping them to acquire good habits in terms of hygiene, personal care, responsibility towards oneself and others, and social etiquettes would not only help them and the family but also enhance their respect and social acceptability. Though the training should begin early and should be consistent, it is never too late to learn.

Parents often underestimate the need for discipline when their children are young. We need to keep in mind that the child is going to grow into an adult and parents too will become old. Good habits and sense of responsibility will help challenged children in becoming well-adjusted and mature adults.

What needs to be highlighted is the fact that the society at large fails to see the strengths of individuals with ID and focuses primarily on their limitations. They have enormous strengths – capacity for love and joy, freedom from biases and prejudices, purity of mind and freedom from egoism, warmth in relationships and perseverance despite difficulties in learning. These strengths must be upheld and nurtured by other significant members of society, including parents, teachers, and community and so on.

In the context of their education, it takes all stakeholders in the system (learners, parents, community, teachers, administrators, and policy makers) to be comfortable with diversity and perceive it as a challenge and opportunity rather than a problem. An inclusive school recognises that pupils with special educational needs have a right to learn and positively acknowledges their efforts and achievements. Inclusive classroom culture encourages positive effort and promotes the idea of learning as a joyful activity. A system where inclusion is practised in an all-encompassing manner sends a lot of positive messages not only to its own members but also to other individuals and institutions.

As noted by Smith, Polloway, Patton & Dowdy (2013), the perspectives around ID have seen a major positive attitudinal shift and the powerful message of the twenty first century is that people with ID are capable of substantial achievements as we help develop their strengths and assets.

Conclusion

The domain of mild and moderate intellectual disability needs to be attended rigorously to inform educational planning and familial practices. Right from an appropriate diagnosis of mild and moderate ID to the inclusion of such children in the mainstream institutions is of paramount importance for their social, psychological and emotional well-being. The same, however, can be achieved with an individual and societal mind-set that views diversity as the law of nature and embraces ID as a challenge and opportunity rather than a problem. A healthy and positive attitude towards persons with intellectual disability (PWID) that focuses on their abilities and seeks way to nurture them is quintessential in creating a conducive environment where concrete interventions may promise to yield results. The family as the first socialising agency can help PWID by creating a safe emotional environment and maintaining a routine with predictable structure and avenues for support when required. The aim should be to improve the academic level of learning and adaptive behavioural skill keeping the inherent limitation characterising mild and moderate ID. Common experiences of parents with children having ID include development of low self-image, grief and frustration which may negatively impact the growth of children with ID and therefore there is a need to create a nexus where support mechanism is available. As compared to children with severe and profound level of ID, the children with mild and moderate ID can well be included in the mainstream schools with modification in curricular structure and instructional methodology. Teachers, however, should work alongside and in collaboration with special educators to cater to the academic learning and psycho-social adjustments of children with mild and moderate ID. Together they can frame learning experiences and assessment suited for individual children. Use of different therapies as suited to the need of individual children can also help the children adjust socially and emotionally.

Therefore, the collective and concerted efforts towards positive parenting and education of children with mild and moderate ID are the need of the hour so that the children with these often neglected and misinterpreted levels of ID can be responded well.

REFERENCES

Mangal, S.K. (2007). *Educating Exceptional Children*, New Delhi: Prentice Hall of India

National Council of Educational Research and Training (2006). *Position paper: Education of Children with special needs*, New Delhi: NCERT

Thomas, C.H. and Patton, J.R. (1990). "Mild and moderate retardation", In: J.R. Patton, J.S. Payne and M.B. Smith (Eds.). *Mental Retardation*, (pp. 197-226), London: Merrill.

Polloway, E.A., Lubin, J., Smith, J.D. and Patton, J.R. (2010). "Mild intellectual disabilities: Legacies and trends", *Education and Training in Autism and Developmental Disabilities*, 45(1): 54-68.

Puri, M. (2004). "Intellectual impairment", M. Puri and G. Abraham (Eds.), *Handbook of Inclusive Education*, (pp. 172-189), New Delhi: Sage.

Smith, T.E.C, Polloway, E.A., Patton, J.R. and Dowdy, C.A. (2012). *Teaching Students with Special Needs in Inclusive Settings*, MA: Pearson.

Web Resources

http://www.do2learn.com/ (November 5, 2017)

http://www.ds-health.com/pueschel.htm (October 15, 2017)

http://mhrd.gov.in/iedss (October 23, 2017)

http://www.muskaanthengo.org/intellectual-disability/defining-understanding-disability/ (October 21 2017)

https://www.unicef.org/disabilities/files/Factsheet_A5_Web_NEW.pdf (November 15, 2017)

5

Locomotor Impairment

Perspectives and Concerns about Inclusion

Sailaja Chennat

Locomotor impairment is defined as a person's inability to execute distinctive activities associated with movement of self and objects, resulting from affliction of musculoskeletal or nervous system or both. (The Schedule in the Rights of Persons with Disability Act, (RPwD Act, 2016). What is implied is that, impairment of mobility can be related to either muscles and bones (orthopaedic) or muscles and nerves (neuromuscular) or both orthopaedic and neuromuscular.

As per the Schedule in the RPwD Act 2016, a person who has been cured of leprosy with restricted movements of hands and legs; a person with cerebral palsy, non-progressive neurological condition affecting body movements and muscle coordination, caused by damage to one or more specific areas of the brain; person with dwarfism; person with muscular dystrophy, hereditary genetic muscle disease that weakens the muscles that move the human body and "acid attack victims" with disfigured body parts caused due to violent assault by throwing of acid or similar corrosive substance, are included under locomotor impairment.

Anyone with locomotor impairment may need medical attention and in certain cases specialised ones. However, the social problems that locomotor impairment poses demand an integrated approach. Persons with locomotor impairment need an affable surrounding, a wholesome ambience which is possible only with the collaborative efforts of many segments of the society, such as doctors, social scientists, engineers, administrators and many others.

Nature of Locomotor Impairment

A person with disability is perceived as 'not normal' or at worst, inferior, to able-bodied peers. Such negative perceptions and stigma invade almost every aspect of our cultural values from the highly graded traits we associate with masculinity and femininity, to beliefs about what is beautiful. The specific challenges people with disabilities face with regard to self-esteem and body image are agreed upon across the globe and are supported with adequate research evidence. At the broadest level, studies have found that impairment related to limbs and body, affecting mobility in particular, has a negative influence on a person's psychological experience, attitudes, and feelings about his/her own body.

Persons with locomotor impairment may have different types and degrees of difficulty in physical movement of either a part of the body or whole body. Most types of locomotor impairment affect the external appearance of a person, especially because most of them are dependent on some sort of assistive device for their mobility or body movements. Unlike other impairments—for example, hearing—this impairment cannot be hidden from view. Being an obvious and hard impairment, it severely impacts a person's body image.

Types of Locomotor Impairment

Locomotor impairment can be classified as: congenital (from birth) and acquired (acquired after birth). Common examples of congenital impairment are cerebral palsy, congenital dislocation of hip, etc. Acquired disability can be due to infections or trauma. Disabilities can be acquired due to any of the following infections: tuberculosis of spine or other joints, chronic osteomyelitis, septic arthritis, acute poliomyelitis, G.B. syndrome, leprosy, encephalitis and AIDS. Disability caused by trauma can be due to any of the following reasons: traffic accidents (air, water, and road), domestic accidents, industrial accidents, agricultural accidents, fall from height, bullet injuries, injuries sustained in explosions or violence, sports injuries, natural catastrophes, such as earthquakes and floods. Metabolism too can be a causative factor as in the case of rickets, diabetes mellitus and gout. There can be degenerative causes too. Examples are: Parkinson's disease, multiple sclerosis, osteoarthritis, spondylitis and muscular dystrophy.

Our focus in this chapter is on children with locomotor impairment and their inclusion in the school system.

Understanding the Concerns of Children with Locomotor Impairment (CwLI)

Social integration, positive self-concept and behavioural adjustment are important dimensions of a child's development. For CwLI, the behavioural, emotional and psycho-social aspects of personality may get affected due to considerable limitation of movements and consequently, access to basic needs. These aspects of development are discussed below.

Lack of Mobility

By definition, CwLI have disorders that affect motor movements. When motor problems affect arms and hands, they may have difficulty in manipulating classroom equipment such as writing tools, keyboard, books, geometry equipment, microscope, dissection equipment or in performing daily living activities, such as having lunch, using washroom, taking off shoes and socks, moving from one venue to another. Even when assistive devices are used, some may work at a slow pace and may fall behind others. For example, a student may learn to use an alternate input device for computer, but may be able to type only three words in a minute. This would negatively impact the ability to write and revise lessons while keeping up with other school work.

Lack of Free Play in Childhood

'Many CwLI are likely not to have had much free play alone or with friends. This deprivation in childhood impacts them in the adolescent phase and adulthood too. Play is considered to be the primary activity of a child, a prerequisite to competence in occupational roles later in life. During play, a child explores the environment for its own sake', Missiuna & Pollock (1991). There is also a skill component emerging from the internal motivation to master the environment. Play and work are viewed along a developmental continuum, with play continuing to serve an adaptive function in adulthood. Free play provides a forum for children to explore their own capacities, to experiment with objects, to make decisions, to understand cause-and-effect relationships, to learn, to persist and to understand consequences. This type of play also fosters creativity and allows a child to develop social skills when the play involves peers. Cotton (1984) suggested that, in addition to developing competence through play, the child also learns to cope with anxiety, frustration and failure. If children with physical disabilities are deprived of the opportunity to regularly engage in free play, it seems plausible that particular types of issues are likely to result, such as increased dependence on others, decreased motivation, lack of assertiveness, lowered self-esteem, etc. (Clarke, Riach, & Cheyne, 1977/1982; Mogford, 1977). These secondary issues have an impact, not only on the child's play and development, but also on later functioning in school, community and society, and workplace.

Lack of Common Experiences

CwLI may lack knowledge of common places due to the difficulty in ambulating and exploring interesting places or engaging in activities. This may become apparent in their poor comprehension of literary readings and materials in other content areas. For example, some students may have never seen an ant since they may not have had an opportunity to typically squat on the ground, or be out in the garden and explore the ground. Lack of common experiences can negatively impact their comprehension of learning materials; it may also result in lower achievement and IQ scores when questions are based on experiences that they have been deprived of. For example, one item on a standardised IQ test asks how to remove a ring stuck on a finger and a student who has no palm selected the picture showing pliers instead of the one showing soap and water. In another test, the student was asked to select a picture illustrating one way we all talk to each other; a student with cerebral palsy picked a calculator instead of a telephone because it looked like the augmentative communication device she had been using (Heller & Jones, 2003).

Intellectual Abilities

A group of CwLI has the same variations in intelligence as any group of children and do not need a special curriculum as they do not have learning, language, perceptual or sensory problems. While two children may have the same diagnoses, they may have very different physical and intellectual capabilities. Students with neuromotor impairments are more likely to have additional impairments if brain damage is involved. Many students with orthopaedic impairments, however, do not have learning, language, perceptual, or sensory problems. Most students with orthopaedic impairments will require some classroom infrastructural modifications and accommodation, and assistive technology to function as independently as possible.

What they need is acceptance, and some physical accommodation. They are capable of contributing as much to the classroom as any other child.

Fatigue and Endurance

Students may have several individual factors, partly due to locomotor impairments, that affect their performance in school. Many of them experience fatigue and endurance related problems due to the effort it takes to move. Fatigue and endurance may also occur as a side effect of medications taken for problems such as seizures. These problems can divert their attention from school tasks and can interfere with learning (Heller & Jones, 2003).

Restricted Communication

Motor impairment can be related to either muscles—bones (orthopaedic) or muscles—nerves (neuromuscular) or both. Children with cerebral palsy (CP), for example, often have communication difficulties. Speech delays, articulation disorders, fluency disorders and voice disorders are common. Children may also have difficulty in producing sounds due to poor muscle control. Many youngsters with CP have dysarthria, a motor speech disorder. Such students with speech impairment can be affected academically due to their inability to fully communicate their ideas or to ask questions for clarification, or to fully participate in the learning activity.

Psychological Factors

CwLI realise as early as preschool that they are different from others and many know the name of their conditions with at least one of its effects by age three or four years (Dunn, McCartan and Fuqua, 1988). How CwLI come to view themselves and their abilities can impact how well they perform in school. Students' negative reactions to their disability may result in feelings of isolation or unhappiness (Rydstrom, Englund and Sandman, 1999). Poor self-concept and self-esteem have also been linked to depression in these children (Kazdin, 1988). These children are found to have less social competence and social support, the two major coping strategies to handle problematic situations and predictors of overall quality of life (Best, 1999).

Body Image

A boy with a defunct right palm with no right fingers is apparently like any other student in the class, may be confident and enthusiastic and may participate well in the group. However, since he does not have full grown right palm or fingers, he is not able to do some tasks including writing with right hand. Not being able to use his right hand for all the tasks that are generally done with the right hand, is something specific to him. His body image, with a very different looking right palm, could scar his self-concept. He uses his left hand to write and hence needs space on his left side. You may have seen children using crutches or wheelchair for mobility. Have you thought of their capabilities in academics and co-curricular activities? What do they feel about body image? What is the level of their self-confidence? Most of the CwLI do not have any cognitive inabilities; in other words, the range of cognitive abilities is as spread out in this group of children as in any other group. What hits them emotionally is the way they look, the image of their body, dependence on crutches, wheelchair or other people for mobility and the fact that while moving in a group often they lag behind.

The link between body image and disability has been proved through a number of research studies. "More and more research has confirmed the unique challenges people with disabilities face with regards to self-esteem and body image. At the broadest level, studies have found that physical disability in particular has a negative influence on people's psychological experience, attitudes and feelings about their own bodies" (Gerber, 2016).

Independence, dominance, strength, athletic appearance with a six-pack body are just some of the twenty attributes and body images associated with masculinity in our society. For young adults and men with physical disabilities, especially where the impairment is obvious and makes them dependent on devices such as wheelchairs, crutches, canes and artificial limbs for mobility, it is difficult to live up to such masculine ideals. This often damages the self-esteem of disabled men, leading them to question their masculinity, their desirability, and their very place in society. The same applies to disabled young girls and women. The ideas of femininity and beauty associated with body image severely affect girls and women with locomotor impairment, especially those who are dependent on assistive devices for mobility.

Case Narration

Mahima was born with a defunct vertebral column and hence could not walk. However, intellectually she was just fine and so her parents were encouraged to admit her in school. She had to be carried to school and her learning was all in lying down posture. She could write and read and this helped her pass from one class to next. When she was thirteen, physical abuse by the person who used to carry her to school brought her ambition of continuing her schooling to a halt. (From the narration of a parent during field work by the author. Name has been changed.

Challenges Faced by CwLI

Considering the diversity of conditions that fall within the category of locomotor impairment, educational challenges will differ case by case, and thus the strategies used in each case should focus on the student's unique needs. Possible academic barriers include:

Non-accessible Transportation

Some of our schools have ramps and wheelchair friendly toilets, but when the public transport system is not congenial for wheelchair users, this adaptation has limited utility. Some of the modern buses have ramps for wheelchairs to be pushed in, which account for less than 2 per cent of the overall number of buses that ply on our roads. Aircrafts have ramps for the convenience of wheelchair users. But neither trains nor buses have this facility. This deprives children using wheelchair of accessing these means of transportation.

Non-accessible School Building

When school buildings do not have ramps, students using wheelchair are deprived of entering the building. Most of the school buildings have two and more floors. If there are no lifts in the building, these children are again disabled even if there are ramps allowing their entry into the building.

Trouble Manoeuvring Around the Classroom

Most of our classrooms are packed with a large number of students sitting in one room. In such cases, children on wheelchairs do not feel comfortable as they need more space to manoeuvre through the classroom. Any group activity that requires changed seating arrangement poses a challenge for them.

Difficulty in Navigating through School Corridors and Pathways

The above point of access applies to this situation too. Corridors and hallways in our schools are often jammed and cluttered making it difficult for students using crutches, canes, and especially wheelchairs, to navigate through.

Difficulty in Participating in Sports and Cultural Activities

During sports activities, most CwLI often stay back in their classes when their friends enjoy sports and games in the playground. Alternative games and leisure activities are usually not planned out for them. The sense of isolation and exclusion that they feel is often not understood well by either their peer group or teachers.

Difficulty in Communicating Effectively

Some of the CwLI with neurological issues may have difficulty in communicating effectively. Dysarthriais a motor speech disorder caused by a neurological injury or disease and it can affect one or more of the speech subsystems—respiration, phonation, resonance, prosody, or articulation.

Low self-image

CwLI who use wheelchair, crutches, cane or walker may have a low self-image due to the obvious difference in their appearance from that of others, their dependence on a support for movement (in most cases), and the experience of lagging behind in a group due to their laboured movement. There is enough literature which proves the link between body image and disability (Refer to 2nd paragraph on page 6).

Addressing the Challenges

The following sections present some of the ways in which the above challenges can be addressed.

Infrastructural Modifications

Ramps for entering the school, lifts to reach the upper floors of the building and special wheelchair friendly toilets are the three basic infrastructural facilities necessary for CwLI, especially those using wheelchair. Transportation facilities for their access to the school building are crucial but they do not fall within the purview of the school system. School administration, Head teachers and teachers need to think about the space required to manoeuvre mobility devices such as wheelchairs, walkers, crutches and canes, when arranging classroom furniture and assigning seats. For example, placing a student who uses a walker close to the classroom's entrance is usually more practical than placing her/him in the middle of the classroom.

Navigating school corridors and other pathways is an issue for those school students who have to move from room to room for their classes throughout the day. While making any educational plan specific to the CwLI, care should be taken to ensure that they do not have to exert themselves physically to participate in any activity. In addition to this, these students can be allotted classrooms near the school's elevator to enable them to travel safely between floors.

Physical Activities

Provisions for physical education should match with the student's specific physical abilities. A CwLI may be able to participate in gym class, while a doctor's note can excuse a student with severe impairment from participating. A Physical Education teacher needs to be sensitive and should take care of such individual differences. There is another aspect to this concern. It is fairly commonplace in our contexts to find a child with locomotor impairment sitting in the classroom when others would be out playing. Teachers in such cases need to be more sensitive and should empathise with CwLI for the feeling of exclusion and isolation experienced by them. They should either make arrangements to enable CwLI to be with other students in the playground so that they can at least see their friends play; alternatively, opportunities for children to express their other strengths should be provided.

Classroom Modifications

CwLI in most cases do not need any curricular modifications. What they do need is modifications in the infrastructure and better access to information for proper inclusion. Although classroom modifications and accommodation will vary as per the individual needs of students, the following list includes some common infrastructural and other modifications which can be introduced in a classroom.

- Special seating arrangements to develop useful posture and aid in movement, larger tables for those who have problems in their posture, as in children with CP
- Note-taking assistance for those who have impairment in wrist and fingers that restrict them from writing
- As many CwLI have problems with gross and fine motor development, instructions focused on the development of gross and fine motor skills are required to enable them to function successfully.
- Securing assistive technology and augmentative communication devices as per the specific needs of CwLI
- Extended time to complete assignments.

Teacher's Role in Psycho-Social Accommodations

To cope with the feeling of inadequacy and low self-concept, CwLI require psycho-social accommodations, in addition to a barrier-free physical environment for easy access to the scholastic and co-scholastic activities. Understanding the psycho-social needs of children with impairments is critical for a teacher to be effective in rendering support to these children. Educators should remember that CwLI should be educated and treated as other students. Awareness of students' conditions and its effect on them (such as fatigue and poor stamina) are vital for effective inclusion of the students. It is very important to make sure that a child using wheelchair is not left with a feeling of isolation when small group activities are organised in the classroom with changed seating arrangements. The social and psycho-social model of disability emphasises the role of the teacher and the peer group in accommodating and supporting children with impairment. As a teacher, knowing their capabilities, interests and aptitude, and boosting their self-concept are critical to fulfilling his/her role as a mentor to these children.

5.5. There could be children who suffer pain constantly, or at frequent intervals or sometimes during the day. Only a sensitive teacher can notice this through sharp observations. It is important to empathise and be patient with such children. Teachers must give them time to take break and relax in between tasks.

Buddy Culture

A CwLI would depend on peers for mobility, learning, writing and other similar tasks according to the type of impairments s/he has. Teachers can counsel the peer group of the child to act as a buddy to her/him, taking turns, if need be, so that the CwLI has a buddy as an escort which makes her/him feel included and part of the class group.

Encouraging Reciprocity

Every child has certain strengths that need to be tapped and enriched. This is one of the important roles of the teacher. CwLI usually get labeled as 'disabled' and draw pity and sympathy from people around who often overlook their many other hidden talents. Being 'disabled' is not the only identity they have. For instance, a child who uses wheelchair due to locomotor impairment can be good at singing, playing an instrument, playing chess, painting, creative writing, some handicrafts. The possibilities are unlimited. It is the role of the school system, including the teachers, peers, school management and other staff members to provide opportunities to uncover and hone the talents in these children. The next stage is to inculcate a culture of reciprocity or symbiotic dynamics in the class so that each child's strengths are made use of and developed by a buddy working with him/her. For example, if there is a CwLI who is good at drawing and another student with a flair for creative writing, assigning to them as a pair, the task of making a chart with creative visuals and texts will make both of them work together in collaboration. This will boost the self-confidence and morale of both, especially the child with impairment. It is important to foster this belief in people that children with impairment have talents that others can depend on.

Peer Counselling

It is common in our context to find peers ridiculing CwLI by using derogatory terms to address them or to talk about them. For example, children who limp or walk with the support of crutches, walker, wheelchair or cane are called ***langda*** in Hindi, meaning lame. Sometimes, they are humiliated for being dependent on others. The severity of the impact of such ridicules and humiliation is seldom understood by the peer group. The damage which such behaviour causes to the self-image and identity of a CwLI is very deep. It is in this context that the role of teachers becomes crucial. Only teachers can counsel peers and make them understand the damaging effects of their taunts and ruthless behaviour on their friends with impairment and how their cooperation is critical to the feeling of well-being in them. Instances of such behaviours need to be observed and handled very carefully by teachers. Such cases of teasing or bullying should be checked immediately followed by counselling sessions.

Case Narration

In the initial days of interaction between a teacher and her students, the boy who came across as an articulate and enthusiastic student, like many other children in his class, did not strike as odd except that he always held his right hand at the back of his body. It was in one of the close interactions that the teacher noticed that he did not have his right palm and fingers. He was seen writing confidently with his left hand. The teacher considered this impairment very lightly, as, after all he was able to write quite well as others with his left hand. She also thought that compared to those with visual impairment and hearing impairment, this impairment was much less disabling. This conception of his impairment was proved to be totally unfounded when she came to know his predicament later in a close personal interaction. His childhood and schooling were very difficult, tarnished by humiliating comments from family members, friends and many others which demoralised him and diminished his self-confidence considerably. As an adolescent when he had to change school due to change of residence, he was hoping for a better environment. He was totally disappointed when he had to face the same treatment which demotivated him from attending school. Gradually his absence from school increased and in Class IX he refused to go to school altogether. What followed was the brilliant intervention and counselling by his father which gradually motivated him to rethink and he decided to continue his education. (from the author's field experience)

The narration above clearly brings out the impact of the attitude of peer group and the timely intervention of parent in the education of a CwLI. Had the peer group been counselled by sensitive and dedicated teachers at the right time, the child in the narration above would not have suffered the mental agony and aversion for school.

Attitude of Parents and Society

Societal attitudes towards a disabled person range from that of pity to sympathy filled charity to that of aversion, except for a very few which show a positive attitude. The negative attitudes of a large number of people impact disabled persons which emotionally undermine their capacity to cope with disability and life in general. In fact, many persons with locomotor impairment admit that they do not feel disabled, but they are forced to feel that they are disabled by the society through their negative behaviours, sympathy or meaningless acts of charity which cause more harm than good.

Attitude of the family exerts a great influence on the disabled person. For example, some parents regard a disabled child as a burden. Consequently, the child develops a feeling of worthlessness. Some parents, on the other hand, pamper such a child so much that he/she becomes completely dependent on parents and/or siblings which subsequently cause frustration in the long run. This negatively impacts their development. Sometimes other members of the family turn jealous of the disabled child for all the care they receive which further results in their isolation.

Case Narration

Geeta is a bright scholar who has completed M.Phil programme. She is a polio afflicted person who walks with the support of crutches. Her path till the M.Phil programme has indeed been very difficult and troublesome... Geeta was afflicted with polio at the age of three which subsequently affected the development of her left leg. This resulted in a very obvious limp while walking and quite early in life she had to start using support for walking. Slowly, she became an introvert, preferred to be with herself and talked less to people around. She became moody and depressed. Her parents tried to bring her out of her cocoon but failed miserably. Gradually, they inferred that she had cognitive impairment and got her admitted into a school for mentally impaired children. It is when her teachers found that her Mathematical and language skills were extraordinary that everyone realised how bright she was! That was the turning point in her life. She started her studies in a regular school where she grew into a bright student and finally earned her M.Phil degree. (Case of one of the scholars known to the author with name changed.)

This narration testifies to a close positive correlation between a positive self-image and a strong sense of identity in a child with locomotor disability and how damaging the ignorance of parents can be for such a child. Because of low self-confidence and self-esteem, a person may feel remorseful or slip into depression which can be misinterpreted as mental impairment leading to a chain of mishaps in his/her life trajectory.

Assistive Devices

Locomotor disability refers to the disability of the bones, joints, nerves and muscles leading to a substantial restriction of movement of limbs or any part of the body. Assistive devices available for persons with locomotor disability include orthotic devices, prosthetic devices, and rehabilitative devices.

Due to the various levels of severity of locomotor impairment, multiple types of assistive devices may be used for various purposes. As with any student with a disability, assistive technology would be needed to enable him/her to access the educational curriculum. For students with locomotor impairments, these fall into two primary categories:

Devices to Access Information

Assistive technology devices used for aiding students to access educational material include:

- Speech recognition software
- Screen reading software
- Augmentative and alternative communication devices (such as communication boards)
- Academic software packages for students with disabilities
- Alternative keyboards and mice
- Word prediction software.

Devices for Positioning and Mobility

These assistive technology devices focus on helping students participate in educational activities. These devices include:

- Canes
- Walkers
- Crutches
- Wheelchairs
- Specialised exercise equipment
- Specialised chairs, desks, and tables for proper posture development.

Orthotic and Prosthetic Assistive Devices

Orthotic and prosthetic devices fall into the category of specific devices that help in moving from one place to another, augmenting the limbs and their missing structures or supporting any defunct part. The orthotic devices primarily include ankle foot orthosis (AFO), knee ankle foot orthosis (KAFO), hip knee ankle foot orthosis (HKAFO), reciprocating gait orthosis (RGO), and smart walker orthosis (SWO). Prosthesis is an artificial extension that replaces a missing body part. Prostheses are typically used to replace parts lost by injury (traumatic) or missing from birth (congenital) or to supplement defective body parts. In addition to the standard artificial limb for everyday use, many amputees have special limbs and devices to aid in the participation in sports and recreational activities.

(i) Orthotic devices include brace, splint, or other artificial external devices used to support limbs or spine or to prevent or assist movement
(ii) Prosthetic limbs or other artificial body parts for locomotion
(iii) Foot-drop spring shoes and other devices for people cured of leprosy.

Some of the above devices demand prolonged rehabilitative services for the body to accept these along with a high level of endurance of pain. Associated with the use of these devices is the critical aspect of body image which can be addressed only by people around with a high level of sensitivity. Empathetic and sensitive support system is vital for successful mobility and living of persons who use these prosthetic and orthotic devices.

Devices mentioned above fall within this categorisation of assistive devices.

Orthotic and Prosthetic Devices

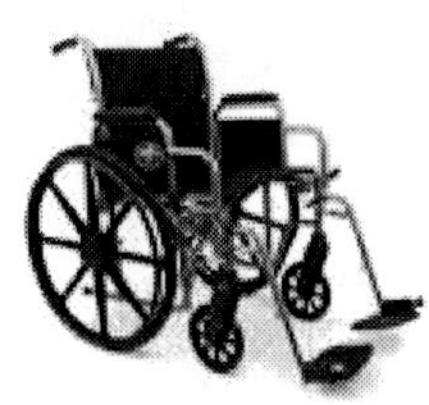		
Wheel Chair	Finger Support	Walker
		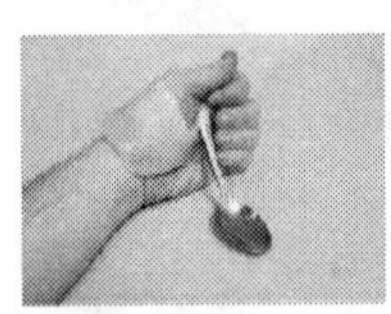
Walker	Full Body Support	Support for Fingers

Source: *peoplehttps://www.google.co.inearch?q=Orthotic+and+Prosthetic+Devices+for+locomotor+impaired+people&tbm=isch&source=lnms&sa=X&ved=0ahUKEwib58uGlaTWAhUDgI8KHRR8DQkQ_AUICigB&biw=1024&bih=613&dpr=1*

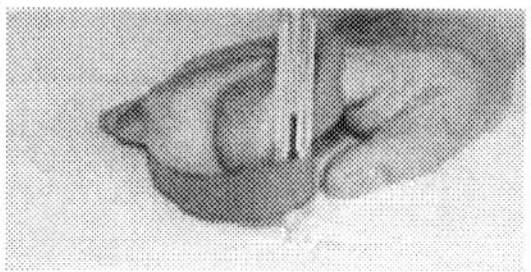

Finger Support

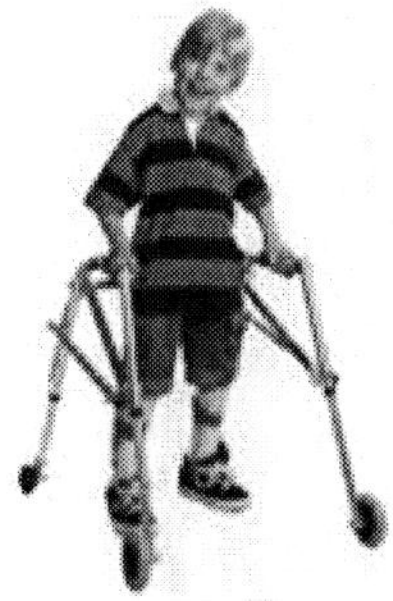

Walker

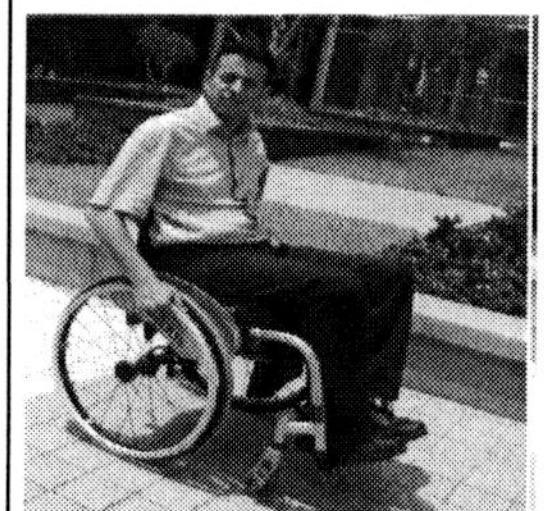

Wheel Chair

Support for Walking

Prosthetic leg

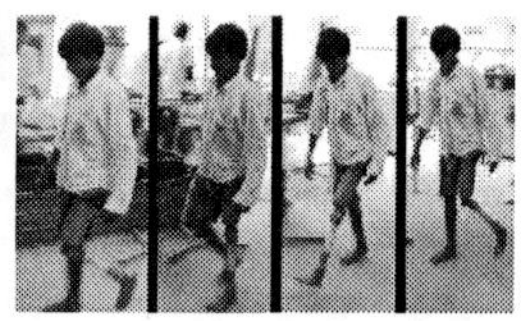

Prosthetic Leg

Prosthetic Leg

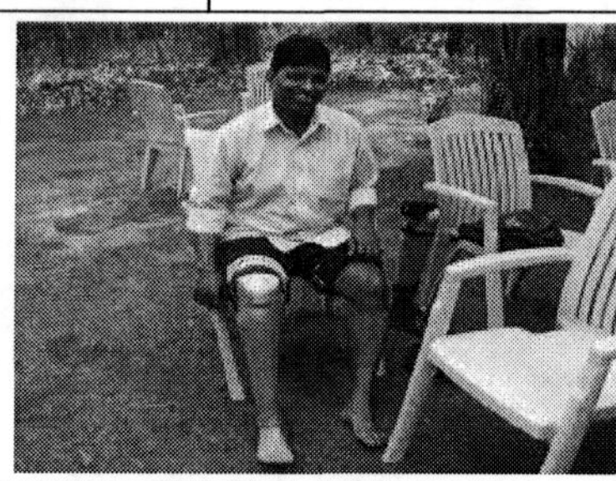

Prosthetic leg: Jaipur Leg

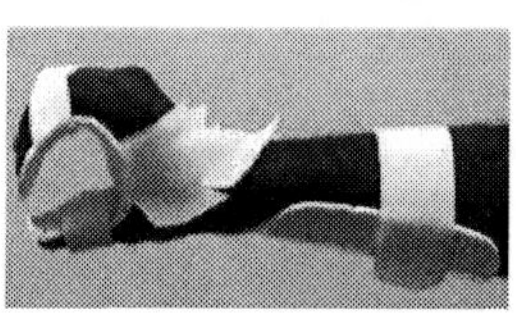

Wrist-hand Positioning Device

Communication Board

Foot drop Spring Shoe (for Leprosy Cured)

Source: *peoplehttps://www.google.co.inearch?q=Orthotic+and+Prosthetic+Devices+for+locomotor+impaired+people&tbm=isch&source=lnms&sa=X&ved=0ahUKEwib58uGlaTWAhUDgI8KHRR8DQkQ_AUICigB&biw=1024&bih=613&dpr=1*

Conclusion

CwLI have difficulty in either moving their body parts or moving from one place to another. Their intellectual ability is as varied as in any group of children. The major problems faced by them relates to access of physical structures and information. Many times, these difficulties hamper their education and professional career. Their impairment being very explicit, leads to low self-confidence and poor body image. Therefore, they need a supportive psycho-social environment for their education and placement. Most of them are helped to a great extent by assistive devices for their mobility and movements of body parts. Assistive technology also helps them to access information. Peer acceptance and social recognition play crucial role in their performance in academics and professional life.

There are many CwLI who have scaled great heights in their academic and professional careers. A brief profile of a few has been presented in the following paragraph.

Sudha Chandran: Famous actress and dancer from Mumbai who has a prosthetic "Jaipur Foot". She is one of the most popular and acclaimed classical dancers of the country. She has also been a known figure in the Indian television and film industry.

Malathy K. Holla: International para-athlete from Bengaluru, was paralysed completely at the tender age of one. She has participated in various international events including the Para-Olympics. She has over 300 medals in her kitty, and is also the proud recipient of the Arjuna Award and Padma Shri. She runs the Mathru Foundation to help disabled children from rural India.

Javed Abidi: Director of the National Centre for Promotion of Employment for Disabled People (NCPEDP) in India, and also the founder of the Disability Rights Group. He was a wheelchair user with Spinabifidia (a developmental congenital disorder caused by the incomplete closing of the embryonic neural tube). (Passed away in 2018)

Arunima Sinha: The first woman amputee to climb Mount Everest with prosthetic leg.

Many others with locomotor impairment have proved that success in life is within their reach despite having an impairment.

Source: https://www.thebetterindia.com/16449/famous-indians-with-7disability/

REFERENCES

Best, S. (1999). "Psychological correlates of physical and health disabilities," In: V.L. Schwean and D.H. Saklofske. (Eds.), *Handbook of Psychosocial Characteristics of Exceptional Children*, NY: Kluwer Academic/Plennum

Clarke, M.M., Riach, J. and Cheyne, W.M. (1982). "Handicapped Children and Pre-School Education." Cited in M. Philip and D. Duckworth (Eds.), *Children with Disabilities and Their Families*. Windsor, England: NFER-Nelson.

Cotton, N. (1984). "Childhood plays an analog to adult capacity to work". *Child Psychiatry and Human Development*. 14: 135-144.

Dunn, N., McCartan, K.W. and Fuqua, R. (1988). "Young children with Orthopedic handicaps: Self-knowledge about their disabilities", *Exceptional Children*, 55: 249-252.

Gerber, C. (2016). *The unique body image challenges related to disability*. https://www.verywell.com/the-unique-body-image-challenges-related-to-disablity-1094483)

Heller, K.W. and Jones, D.S. (2003). "Supporting the educational needs of students with orthopedic impairment", *Physical Disabilities: Education and Related Services*, 22(1): 3-24.

Kazdin, A.E. (1988). *Children's depression*. E.J. Mash and L.G. Terdal (Eds.), Behavioural assessment of childhood disorders (157-195). NY: Guilford.

Missiuna, C. and Pollock, N. (1991). "Play Deprivation in Children with Physical Disabilities: The Role of The Occupational Therapist in Preventing Secondary Disability", *The American Journal of Occupational Therapy*, 45(10): 882-888.

Mogford, K. (1977). *The play of handicapped children*. B. Tizard and D. Harvey (Eds.), Biology of play (pp. 170-184). London: Spastics International.

Rydstrom, I., Englund, A. and Sandman, P. (1999). "Being a child with asthma", *Pediatric Nursing*, 25, 589-596.

Web Resources

RPwD Act: http://www.ncpedp.org/sites/all/themes/marinelli/documents/Rights%20of%20Persons%20with%20Disabilities%20 (RPWD)%20Act%202016.pdf

Web Resources for Images of Assistive Devices

Assistive Devices for Orthopedically Disabled https://images.search.yahoo.com/search images;_ylt=A0SO8ya1Q85Zb.MAd9NXNyoA;_ylu=X3oDMTEyOWw5Y3RzBGNvbG8DZ3ExBHBvcwMxBHZ0aWQDQjQyMTRfMQRzZWMDc2M?p=orthotic+and+prosthetic+devices+for+orthopedically+disabled+people&fr=tightropetb

Jaipur Leg

https://images.search.yahoo.com/search/images;_ylt=A0SO81V9RM5ZPSwABjdXNyoA;_ylu=X3oDMTE0OGQyM2w3BGNvbG8DZ3ExBHBvcwMxBHZ0aWQDQjQyMTRfMQRzZWMDcGl2cw—?p=jaipur+leg&fr2=piv-web&fr=tightropetb

Weighted Vests

http://www.education.com/reference/article/orthopedic-impairments/ (retrieved on 10.11.16)

Modified Writing Aids

https://www.google.co.in/search?q=modified+writing+aids+for+children+with+disability&biw=1366&bih=662&source=lnms&tbm=isch&sa=X&ved=0ahUKEwiE-_rLir_QAhUMt48KHT97CmcQ_AUIBigB (Retrieved on 23.11.16)

Recommended Reading and Video

https://sites.google.com/site/specialeducationnation/orthopedic-impairment
https://www.youtube.com/watch?v=9fJVqWMlDJU
https://www.youtube.com/watch?v=9fJVqWMlDJU (Prof. Anita Ghai's Lecture in 2018 in JNU, Delhi)

6

Specific Learning Disabilities

Issues and Solutions for Inclusion

Sumita Bhangu

"No other disabling condition affects so many people and yet has such a low public profile and low level of understanding as LD," Washington Summit 1994 (Reid L, *et al.*, 1994). Morgan, a general practitioner in Sussex, England, published the first case of what is now known as dyslexia, a word derived from the Latin word "dys", which translates to 'difficult', and the Greek word "lexia", which translates to 'words'; it literally means "difficulty with words".

On 7 November 1896, Morgan wrote in the British Medical Journal, about Percy F., a 14-year old, who was intelligent, bright, quick with learning games, and the intellectual equal of his peers, but fell behind, in his inability to learn how to read.

The term learning disability was coined by Samuel Kirk in a 1963 address to a group of parents whose children were experiencing serious difficulties in learning to read, were hyperactive or could not solve math problems. Numerous definitions have been proposed, but none has been universally accepted. Two definitions that have had the most influence are: the federal definition of Individuals with Disabilities Education Act (IDEA) and the definition proposed by National Joint Committee on Learning Disabilities (NJCLD).

According to the definition of learning disabilities in the federal law IDEA-2004, (Individuals with Disabilities Education Act of USA) 'the term "specific learning disability" (SLD) means a disorder in one or more of the basic psychological processes involved in understanding or in using language, spoken or written, which disorder may manifest itself in imperfect ability to listen, think, speak, read, write, spell or to do mathematical calculations. This term includes such conditions as perceptual disabilities, brain injury, minimal brain dysfunction, dyslexia and developmental aphasia. Such terms do not include a learning problem that is primarily the result of visual, hearing or motor disabilities, of mental retardation, of emotional disturbance, or of environmental, cultural or economical disadvantages'.

Research indicates that despite average or above average intelligence, children with SLD face problems in learning as fast and as accurately as their peer group. This disability is detected primarily in visual and language processing areas, such as reading, writing, speaking, listening, decoding or using symbols. Children with SLD may face problems in connecting sound with the word, learning and writing alphabets, rhyming words or following verbal cues. In India, no nationwide survey on SLD is available but studies by individual researchers have shown that near about 10 per cent children are identified with learning disabilities in Indian schools (Padhy, 2010). In the research study done by NIPCCD (National Institute of Public Cooperation and Child Development) on Scholastic Backwardness (Thapar *et al.*, 2003), learning disabilities was the highest contributory factor of scholastic backwardness with the figure of 64.10 per cent and can be called a major factor for school dropout at primary and elementary stages.

Causes of Specific Learning Disability (SLD)

In most cases, the etiology (cause) of a child's learning disability is unknown. Many causes have been suggested, which probably reflects the highly diverse nature of students with SLD. Factors that affect the brain are many and varied and these include the effect of damage that results from the intake of toxic substances such as drugs, alcohol, certain minerals, and early deprivation, poor nutrition and oxygen deprivation. These can affect in the prenatal (before delivery), perinatal (during delivery) and postnatal (after birth) stages. No single factor or group of factors has been identified as directly causing learning disability. Four suspected causal factors are brain damage, heredity, biochemical imbalance and environmental causes.

Brain Damage or dysfunction: Some professionals believe that all children with SLD suffer from some type of brain injury or dysfunction of the central nervous system. Indeed this belief is inherent in the National Joint Committee on Learning Disabilities (NJCLD) definition of LD, which states that learning disabilities are presumed to be due to the dysfunction of the central nervous system. Another study suggests that it could be due to the maturational delay within the neurological system. Brain damage can also occur due to prolonged labour, post birth trauma, head injury, and lead positioning, seizures and so on.

Heredity: Siblings and children of persons with reading disabilities have a slightly greater than normal likelihood of having reading problems. There is growing evidence that genetics may account for at least some cases of dyslexia. Genetic factors seem to operate in large number of cases.

Behavioural Manifestations

The case of child X presented in the box below is an example of characteristics of SLD.

> X is a student studying in primary grade. She tries to be friendly/social with her peer group but is not able to. She is not interested in studies. According to her parents and teachers, there is a discrepancy between her potential and achievement. At times she becomes very aggressive and irritable or prefers to sit alone. Her difficulties are not the result of any other known condition that can cause learning problems. After clinical assessment it was found that she had SLD.

Students with SLD exhibit many kinds of learning and behavioural traits, and no individual displays all the traits. Some students have disabilities in Mathematics, whereas others excel in Mathematics. Attention disorders are symptomatic problems for many students with SLD, but not for all. Further, certain kinds of characteristics are more likely to be exhibited at a certain age. Young children are more likely to be hyperactive than adolescents. In addition, deficits are manifested in different ways at different age levels. For example, an underlying language disorder may appear as a delayed speech problem in the preschooler, as a reading disorder in the elementary school pupil and as a writing disorder in the secondary school student (Lerner, 2006).

SLDs are associated with problems in listening, reasoning, memory, attention, selecting and focusing on relevant stimuli and the perception and processing of visual and/or auditory information. These difficulties in perceptual and cognitive processing are manifested through one or more of the following characteristics:

- problems in reading (dyslexia),
- deficits in written language (dysgraphia),
- underachievement in Maths (dyscalculia),
- poor social skills, attention deficit, hyperactivity and behavioural problems (Lerner, 2006).

Today all these are included under the umbrella of Specific Learning Disability (SLD). Hence using the word dyslexia, dysgraphia or dyscalculia interchangeably with SLD is technically incorrect. It is important to remember that a Specific Learning Disability, as the name suggests, includes difficulties in specific processing areas as opposed to global difficulties in children with compromised intelligence (Karanth, 2002).

Child with SLD

- Is intelligent but fails in school
- Writes ***'on'*** for ***'no'***, ***'was'*** for ***'saw'***, ***'14'*** for ***'41'*** etc. (**mirror images**).
- Hears the barking of a dog at a distance but does not hear what the teachers say
- Able to recall sequence of TV serial but does not remember tables
- Is confused between yesterday, today and tomorrow
- Has mood swings and is disorganised and messy
- Has poor time management
- Is enthusiastic about finishing particular task in academics but it comes out all wrong
- Omits (reads ***belt*** as ***bet***), adds (***ischool*** for ***school***) or skips words while reading.
- Is not able to sustain attention on a given task for a specific duration of time
- Does not know how to act and talk in social situations.
- Has difficulty with establishing satisfying social relationships and friendships.

Source: RCI study material.

Dyslexia

Dyslexia is a specific learning disability that is neurobiological in origin. It is characterised by difficulties in accurate and/or fluent word recognition and poor spelling and decoding abilities. Decoding is the ability to match letters to sounds and then use that skill to read words accurately and fluently. Children have difficulty in decoding because they often struggle with a more basic language skill called phonemic awareness. One potential sign of dyslexia is when child avoid reading, both out loud and to themselves. Child may even get anxious or frustrated when reading.

Source: https://www.nessy.com/uk/files/2015/02/featured-phonological-dyslexia.jpg

During my work as a special educator at primary level, I have observed that readers with dyslexia tend to be spatially-disoriented, with pronounced confusion between left and right. This affects the way they perceive words. As a result, there is a frequent reversal of letters, for example, ***pot*** for ***top***. Research has shown that phonemic awareness is important to read successfully. Phonemic awareness skills are prerequisites for benefiting from phonics instruction. They are also an important factor in learning how to spell. Teachers can also teach sight words to the learner.

Sight words are commonly used words and with practice, should be identified by sight. They are often referred to as 'high-frequency words.' After all, roughly half of the words in most reading texts are the same words—sight words. There are two widely known sight word lists used by educators, each sectioned by grade-level and ability. These lists were developed separately by education experts Dr. Edward B. Fry and Dr. Edward William Dolch. They share many common words such as 'and,' 'make,' 'where' and 'see. The Dolch Word List of 220 words includes the most frequently used words in the English language. Sight words make up **50 to 70** per cent of any general text. *www.k5learning.com/free-flashcards/reading/dolch*

Dysgraphia

Dysgraphia is the specific learning disability that affects a person's handwriting and fine motor skills. Problems may include illegible handwriting, inconsistent spacing and poor spatial planning on paper, poor spelling and difficulty in composing writing as well as thinking and writing at the same time. They have problem with their grip on the pencil and write very slowly. Their notes are usually incomplete. They generally face problem in copying from the blackboard. They may write letters in a word in wrong order or use mirror images, and thus misspell words such as ***bat*** for ***pat, sun*** for ***son***. They may invert letters such as **u** and **n**. They may also face difficulty in writing words that are pronounced different from their spelling as they spell words the way they sound. For example, ***busy*** may be spelt as ***bizzy*** or ***neighbour*** as ***nebor***.

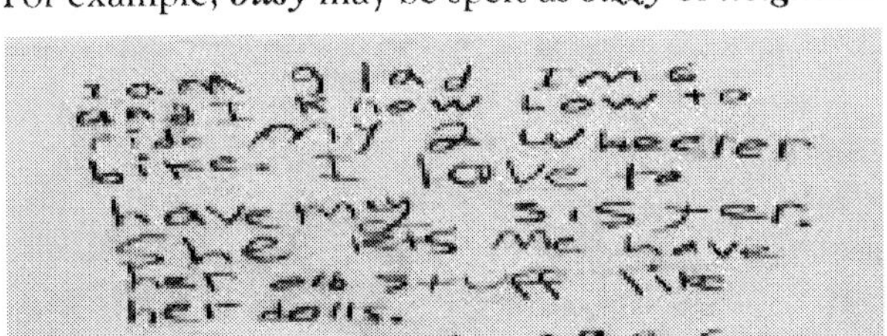

Source: *https://www.medbridgeeducation.com/blog/wp-content/uploads/2016/01/1-8-Jenny-Clark-Dysgraphia-700x2901.png*

An individual with SLD faces significant difficulty in producing neat, legible and expressive written work within certain duration of time. Above is the sample of writing of a child with dysgraphia.

A child with dysgraphia may:

- have odd wrist, body and paper position
- have poor organisation on the page
- have poor right /left orientation
- show inconsistencies, such as mixture of print and cursive, upper and lower case or irregular size, shape or slant of letters
- hold pen/pencil very close to the paper with tight grip which often leads to tearing of paper.
- have illegible printing and cursive writing (despite appropriate time and attention given the task)
- have unfinished words or letters, omitted words
- show inconsistent spacing between words and letters
- exhibit strange wrist, body or paper position
- be slow in copying or writing
- show poor spatial planning on paper
- have cramped or unusual grip/may complain of sore hand
- have great difficulty thinking and writing at the same time (taking notes, creative writing).

Source: RCI study material

Handwriting is a complex perceptual motor skill which requires visual and kinesthetic feedback to execute correct movements. When a child makes a very poor copy of a pattern, it may not be because the visual discrimination required is beyond him, but because he/she may have impaired perceptual motor performance. These children cannot make their hands do what their eyes see.

Dyscalculia

Dyscalculia is the inability to understand numbers and learn Mathematics. Individuals with this type of SLD may have poor comprehension of math symbols, may struggle with memorising and organising numbers, have difficulty telling time, or have trouble with counting. Some children with learning disability use fingers for calculating even after they are over eight years of age. They confuse different symbols and have problems in remembering tables. They have problem in understanding statement problems and deciding on operations. They may also arrive at the correct answer, but when they write they commit mistakes. They make errors such as writing **679** as **976** and make errors generally while copying from rough to fair sheet.

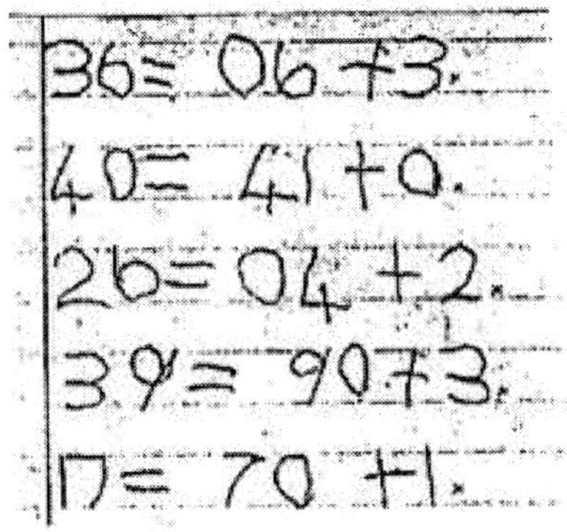

Source: *http://theabsolutevalueofmike.weebly.com/uploads/1/8/6/8/18684912/1365122650.jpg*

Social Skills Deficits

A study conducted by Kavale and Forness (1996) claims that about 75 per cent of students with learning disabilities exhibit deficits in social skills. Poor social skills often lead to rejection, low social status, fewer positive interactions with teachers, difficulty in making friends and loneliness; all of these are experienced by many students with learning disabilities regardless of classroom placement. The poor social skills of students with learning disabilities may be due to inability to perceive emotions of others, specifically nonverbal expressions. Some students with learning disabilities face difficulty in attending to a task and/or display meaningless movement (ADD/ADHD).

Our world is a social place and we spend most of our time participating as members of social groups, such as school, church, neighbourhood, Parent-Teacher Organisations, recreational sports leagues and more. For children, social skills are the foundation for getting along with others from the earliest age. In the case of special needs students and those with SLD, extra help is often needed. Social situations can be complicated for children with social challenges. They often get lost in a maze of limited social understanding. These social skills can be as simple as saying "hello" and "goodbye" and as complicated as knowing how to function in a group setting or during difficult social interactions. Students with social challenges require direct instruction, with each step of every skill broken down into small pieces.

Disorders of Attention

Students with SLD may have attention related problems. They may not focus when a lesson is being presented, have a short attention span, get easily distracted, and have poor concentration. They may also be hyperactive or impulsive. Students with SLD showing the above characteristics may have coexisting attention deficit disorders (ADD).

Poor Motor Abilities

Some children with SLD have difficulty with gross motor abilities and fine motor coordination. They exhibit general awkwardness and clumsiness and have spatial problems. Visual-spatial processing is the ability to tell where objects are in space. That includes one's own body parts. It also involves being able tell how far objects are from oneself and from each other. Visual-spatial processing, in combination with visual-motor skills, lets people coordinate their movements with what they see. For example, to catch a ball, a child must gauge the speed and distance of the ball in flight and adjust her movements accordingly. Children use visual-spatial processing skills to walk through a crowded room without bumping into anyone. Tying a shoelace makes use of visual-spatial processing skills. The visual-spatial part of the task involves understanding how the two laces must be looped together, using both the left and right hand.

Psychological Process Deficits and Information-Processing Problems

Children with SLD often have problems in processing auditory or visual information. For example, many of them are poor in recognising the sounds of language (phonological awareness), in quickly recognising letters or words (visual perception), or in short term memory tasks. We collect information in many ways, including through sight, smell, hearing, taste and touch. The information is known as *input*. But that is only the first step in information processing. Once we gather that data, our brain has to recognise, understand and store it. When we respond to that information, it is called *output*. Output is what we write, say, or do in reaction to the input. Information processing refers to the entire process. It is how the input and output work together. This makes it possible for children to manage various tasks ranging from reading a book to tying shoelaces.

Issues pertaining to information processing arise when a child has trouble with either the input or the output, or both. Having these issues has nothing to do with either the effort or the smartness of the child. Information processing issues reflect how the child's brain is recognising and using the information it received. Any area responsible for information processing may be affected, but some critical ones which are related to learning are: visual processing and auditory processing.

Visual processing refers to how a child uses the data he sees. It involves how quickly he can understand something when he sees it and how well he remembers that information. A child with problem in visual information processing may have trouble in accurately making sense of what he sees. He may lack visual-spatial skills.

S/he may also:

- Find it hard to perceive the differences between similar-looking shapes or letters, such as O and Q
- Have trouble comparing and understanding differences between certain colours, shapes and patterns
- Struggle to locate something specific on a page
- Skip lines or read the same line repeatedly while reading
- Find it hard to write on or between the lines when writing
- Have trouble copying information from the board
- Bump into things or people and have trouble navigating new places

Auditory processing refers to how children use the data they hear. It involves how they make sense of the sounds they hear and how they keep up with the information. Children with difficulties in auditory information processing have trouble making sense of and getting meaning from what they hear. It becomes even more difficult if there is a lot of noise around. Not all children with problems in a particular area of information processing will have the same difficulties.

They may:

- Find it hard to tell the difference between similar-sounding words, such as *fifty* and *fifteen*
- Struggle to understand spoken language
- Have trouble following directions
- Find it hard to remember details they have heard
- Appear as though they are not listening

Screening and Assessment

Why do we need to label a child? It is very important because it helps educators to understand the actual status of the child. In India, parents do not accept labels easily as they consider any label with disability as social stigma. As mentioned above, at times teachers, due to lack of knowledge, fail to understand the real needs of the child. For children who have minor problems in reading, writing or Maths, the screening can be done in the regular classroom. It is only after thorough observations that children, who are suspected to be "at risk' or identified as having SLD, should be sent for screening by specialists so that they can be helped with specialised care.

SLD is different from many other developmental disabilities as it surfaces only during academic performance. In other aspects such as language, intelligence, motivation and behaviour, children with SLD may be at par with other children. This makes early identification and diagnosis of children with SLD a major problem. Only in cases where there is an executive function deficit (problem in planning, organisation and integration) or delay in language development, SLD may be identified early.

The diagnosis of SLD is itself a time-consuming process and a child cannot be labeled as learning disabled without exhausting all efforts to help the child to come out of his/her reading, writing listening and comprehension related difficulties. Failure in academic achievement during initial years cannot be attributed to learning disability. Children should not be labeled as learning disabled unless and until they are at least seven years of age or have completed at least two years of schooling. This implies that diagnosis for learning disability should only be carried out after proper attempts at instruction have been made. Most of the symptoms that surface in learning disability are a part of normal literacy acquisition process in the early years of education. Identification of learning difficulties and providing remediation and alternate learning strategies is the first step towards helping a child in early literacy. It is only when no improvement is made that a child can be considered for diagnosis of learning disability. In such cases where the existence of a SLD cannot be established but the child is facing difficulties, the child is identified as "at risk", with appropriate interventions being initiated.

There are many early warning signs which can alert parents and teachers towards possibility of learning disability in children. Any type of school related problem such as the child refusing to go to school or reluctance to do homework can be a sign of difficulty in learning. Parents or teachers may feel that the child has poor memory, or is lazy or has a dislike for writing, whereas the actual reason may lie hidden due to the child's inability to explain his/her problems. Children do not actively seek help by themselves. It is important for parents and teachers to talk to them and try to find out the reasons behind stress or anxiety in them. Some children might show withdrawal symptoms or make psychosomatic complaints such as recurrent headaches and recurrent stomach aches when pressed to do academic tasks. This is due to the anxiety which these tasks cause them. In adolescents, behavioural problems, substance abuse or high risk behaviours can be due to the academic stress and anxiety caused by learning disability.

If a child shows the above symptoms, clinical psychologists and mental health practitioners can be approached who are qualified to conduct tests and assessment for the identification of LD. There are various types of tools such as checklists and rating scales, parent interviews, informal or natural observations and formal assessments, which can be used for identification of learning disability. Teachers, counsellors and special educators in schools can also be trained to conduct some basic screening tests such as Specific Learning Disability Test (by NIMHANS), Diagnostic Test for Learning Disability (DTLD by SNDT, Mumbai) and curriculum based measurement tool, Grade Level Assessment Device (GLAD) (by NIMH, Hyderabad), which have been devised for Indian population.

Dyslexia Screening Test—Junior, India Edition (DST): DST-J is a powerful screener, developed for use with school children in India in order to identify those who are at the risk of dyslexia. The DST-J replaces the best-selling DST and reflects changes in theory and practice since the initial publication with additional subtests, validation studies and case histories. The Indian norms will not only facilitate a more precise measure of literacy skills but will also provide increased opportunities to a greater number of children to be screened at an early age for the risk of Dyslexia.

The Dyslexia Screening Test series are scientific tests used globally in educational settings to help identify children with Dyslexia. Early identification of Dyslexia will result in timely and effective intervention that will help children cope with it better and prepare them for better academic and professional lives.

Assistive Technology used by Educators: Assistive technology (AT) is available to help individuals with many types of disabilities—from cognitive difficulties to physical impairments. The use of technology to enhance learning is an effective approach. AT for children with SLD is defined as any device, equipment or system that helps bypass, work around or compensate for an individual's specific learning deficits. Over the past decade, a number of studies have demonstrated the efficacy of AT for individuals with SLD. AT does not cure or eliminate learning difficulties, but it can help children reach their potential as it allows them to capitalise on their strengths and helps bypass areas of difficulty. For example, a student who struggles with reading but who has good listening skills might benefit from listening to audio books.

AT can address many types of learning difficulties. A student who has difficulty in writing can compose a school report by dictating it and having it converted into a text by special software. A child who struggles with Maths can use a hand-held calculator to keep score while playing a game with a friend.

Certain AT tools can help people with difficulties in processing and remembering spoken language. Such devices can be used in various settings, e.g., a class lecture, or a meeting with multiple speakers. There is a wide range of AT tools available to help individuals who struggle with reading. While each type of tool works a little differently, all of these tools help by presenting text as speech. These tools help facilitate decoding, reading fluency, and comprehension.

Similarly, a number of AT tools help students who struggle with writing. A gripper can be used to achieve proper pincer-grasp. The image below shows wrong grasp and the one following it shows grippers. Boarders can be used to give cues to students regarding where to start and stop.

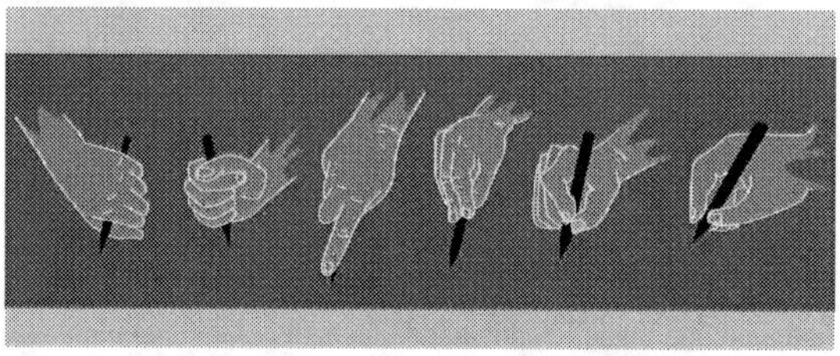

Source: https://www.medbridgeeducation.com/blog/wp-content/uploads/2016/01/1-8-Jenny-Clark-Dysgraphia-700x2901.png

Source: https://childdevelopment.com.au/wp-content/uploads/bfi_thumb/grips-n04qpzrqt426i2c4cugjh82vpu6e60jxctnalm8z1s.jpg

Role of Parent-teacher Collaboration in the Inclusion of SLD

Inclusive education stands for the belief that all children can learn and that all teachers can teach. It emphasises that effective pedagogy needs to be evolved regularly and frequently in order to respond to the ever changing needs of learners. All skills and intelligences need to be assessed. Inclusive education highlights the importance of a nurturing environment in the growth and development of a child where the support and participation of all stakeholders—learners, teachers, parents, community, administrators and policy makers—is crucial.

As reflective practitioners, we need to engage in the cycle of thinking, analysing, rethinking, modifying and implementing. At a deeper level, we must try answering questions such as 'do we as teachers believe that all children learn?', 'what do we mean by learning?', 'what do we mean by education?', 'is it only academics?' With every question answered, teachers need to analyse their words and inquire into the underlying assumptions.

Teachers must:

- break learning into small steps;
- administer probes;
- supply regular and quality feedback;
- use diagrams, graphics and pictures to augment what they say in class;
- provide ample independent and well-designed intensive practice;
- model instructional practices that they want students to follow;
- provide prompts for strategies to be used by students; and
- engage students in process type questions, such as "How is the strategy working? Where else you might apply it?"

Inclusion is the only way forward for children with learning disability. SLD is one of the main major causes behind dropout in school enrolment after elementary school. Psychologists state that assistance to children with SLD must be carried on in a non-medical model. Such children should not be segregated rather they should be provided an environment that encourages them to realise their potential. The school environment should be modified in a manner that it becomes responsive to learners' individual differences and diversity in a more constructive manner. The curriculum should be flexible enough to take into account the special needs of children with learning difficulties. To help learners with learning difficulties, psychologists and teachers need to work in tandem to plan and conduct remedial classes and create alternative assessment strategies.

The first step in moving towards inclusion of children with SLD is to make teachers aware about learning disabilities, child development and child psychology. It is only when they are well informed that they can identify children who show early symptoms of learning difficulty. There are some screening tests available which can be used for diagnosis. Teachers can be trained to do the first round of screening. If children with learning difficulties are identified early, they can be put in remedial classes. It has been observed that most students who are not learning disabled can improve with these initial interventions.

The secondary characteristics associated with SLD are low motivation, negative and critical attitude towards self and others, poor self-esteem and other emotional and behavioural issues. Unfortunately, teachers as well as parents tend to concentrate more on behavioural problems and forget the core issue. There is a need to sensitise teachers towards such problems. Teachers who are aware and are empathetic towards children with SLD know that they should not brand these children as 'lazy' or 'stupid', should not punish them for minor mistakes and ensure that they are not bullied or teased by other children.

> *Examples*
>
> A mother of a child with SLD shares her concern that her child who is an VIIIth grader did not do anything in the classroom because her class-teacher did not allow him to do so. If he tried to be a part of an ongoing activity, he was sent to the special education room. He was not allowed to be part of the class. She further says that in the next year the school would not let him pass to IXth standard because according to the school system it would affect their school result.
>
> A parent asks a teacher. "Ma'am please let me know when you are taking leave; I won't send my child to school because in that situation he will sit idle in class".

Teachers can engage children with SLD in the learning process by using modified strategies to evaluate them and by emphasising the learning process more than achievement on end result. Teachers must make preferential seating arrangements and give such learners extra time and assistance to complete tasks. They must also provide them assistance to complete written work or ask their peers to do so. Teachers must ignore minor errors such as spelling errors in their written work. These strategies can help boost confidence of children with SLC and motivate them to work.

Scaffolding is a process that makes a lot of difference. The teacher can start out by using heavily mediated instruction, known as explicit instruction, and then slowly let the students acquire the skill, moving towards the goal of student mediated instruction. Success for students with learning disabilities requires a focus on individual achievement, individual progress, and individual learning. This necessitates the use of specific, directed, individualised and intensive remedial instruction for students who are struggling. Whether the student is in the general education classroom or in a special class setting,

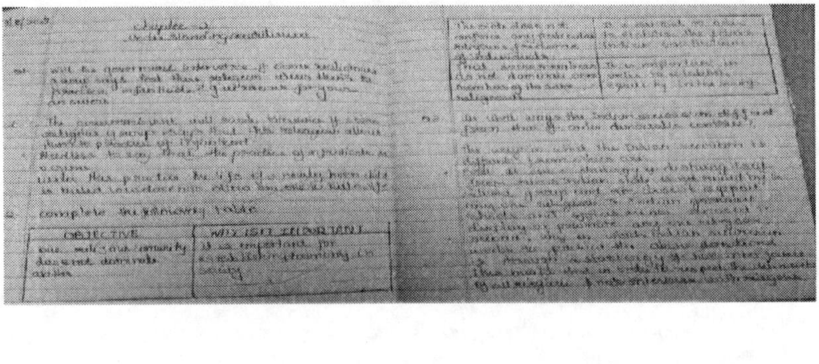

focus of the activities should be on assessing individual students to monitor their progress. Concern for the individual must take precedence over concern for the group or the curriculum or for the organisation and management of the general education classroom content.

The picture above depicts one such example of a teacher who has ignored minor errors of spelling and punctuation and has focused on the overall conceptual understanding of the student.

Such practices assist children with learning disability to continue their education despite limitations. These children may not be able to perform each task given to them accurately, but even while making mistakes they are able to gain knowledge and remain engaged in the learning process.

Teachers should try to include new and varied methods of teaching and carrying out assessment. They should try to use alternative strategies such as oral and written instructions, provide copies of lecture notes, allow the use of tape recorders, laptops, calculators and provide visual and auditory aids in order to become more inclusive. Schools can help children with learning disabilities by making their practices more flexible. Children with SLD can be very slow in writing and may take a lot of time to complete their classwork. Teachers need to be more cooperative, patient and should assist students whenever required. The school should provide additional support to these children during exams by reading out aloud the question paper to the child so that she/he can comprehend and write.

Many children develop fear of particular subjects. There is a tendency among teachers and parents to motivate children to learn certain subjects such as Mathematics by instilling fear in them. They pass judgements by making statements, such as "you are not intelligent if you fail in Maths". For children with dyscalculia, such negative comments hamper their learning and aggravate their fears. Schools can help by changing their outlook towards the learning process and encourage the child to engage with Mathematics even if they are unable to reach the "correct" answer. The main idea is that children with dyscalculia should not feel left out or suffer from low self-esteem.

Children with SLD have difficulty in understanding instructions. They are not able to comprehend what is said to them. They should be given them clear instructions for every task.

> Rohin wanted to play with Shishir, so he picked him up while playing. When the teacher saw this, she said, "Rohin, leave him." Immediately, Rohin dropped Shishir (taking teacher's command literally). If the teacher had said, 'put him down', then he would have put him down, instead of just dropping him abruptly.

Social Stories: A social story is a frequently used strategy to teach social skills to children with disabilities. A social story is a non-coercive approach that presents social concepts and rules to children in the form of a brief story.

This strategy could be used to teach a number of social and behavioural concepts, such as making transitions, playing a game, and going on a field trip. Carol Gray (1995; 2000) outlines a number of components that are essential to a successful social story: the story should be written in response to the child's personal need; the story should be something the child wants to read on her own (depending upon ability level); the story should be commensurate with the ability and comprehension level of the children; and the story should use less directive terms such as "can" or "could" instead of "will" or "must". This last component is especially important for children who tend to be oppositional or defiant (i.e., the child who does not decide what to do until you tell him to do something and then he does the opposite!). The social story can be paired with pictures and placed on a computer to take advantage of the child's inclination towards visual instruction and interest in computers.

Peer Tutoring: Along with social stories, teachers can use peer tutoring in a regular classroom. Peer tutoring in special education is a strategy where higher performing students are paired with lower performing students or students with disabilities to review or teach academic material. This strategy has been proven to help students on both sides to master content and gain self-confidence in specific skills. Peer tutoring has been implemented with students of all ages and levels in all subject areas (where). For example: Teacher can pair a child having poor social skills with a child who is good in social skills. I use this technique in my classroom teaching where I made a pair of two students: one special need student (very good in spellings) but need constant reminders to behave well, another who is very good at social skills but not so good in spellings. After using this method for over a period of time positive changes are visible enough in both students. Introducing a peer tutoring programme to help students with disabilities and their peers may be an effective and efficient way to boost academic achievement. Teachers and administrators should consider the different ways of implementing such a programme and its advantages and weaknesses in their schools and classrooms.

Advantages of Peer Tutoring:

- Peer tutors become teachers, which increases their own understanding of the material.
- Peer tutoring helps students build relationships, which further build communication and social skills.
- Some students with disabilities respond better to peers than adults.
- Students with disabilities get more individual attention than one teacher can provide in their classroom.
- Because of increased individual attention, students with disabilities receive feedback and positive reinforcement more frequently, which results in higher academic performance.

Challenges Ahead

Finally, there is a need to bring more flexibility and changes in the evaluation processes. Children with learning disabilities are capable of performing well at school when given adequate opportunities. They can be given exemptions in different areas such as learning a third language, Mathematics in case of dyscalculia and using the help of a scribe during examination. Their question paper can be modified in a manner which gives ample choices in questions to be attempted. Since they face problems in writing long answers, teachers must use multiple choice questions and short answer questions for assessment. They should also be given extra time to complete examination because they are much slower than the rest of the children.

The near total lack of alternate systems of education and the social premium on a handful of vocational courses with an utter disregard for many others are some of the major hurdles in the 'education' of children with LD. These are but some of the issues faced by the individual and the family of the learning disabled, to date in India (Karanth, 2002).

Conclusion

SLD is a high incidence disability and manifest in cognitive deficit in areas such as reading, writing, mathematical ability and number sense. Children with SLD may also have problem related to attention span, motor coordination, visual processing and auditory processing. The diagnosis of SLD is particularly complicated as many cases of SLD become noticeable during academic performance. Any child may have issues related to reading and writing and arithmetic in the initial stages of learning. Thus, it is crucial to take thorough measures to respond to the difficulties the child is facing in the areas of language or arithmetic before decisively concluding that he/she has SLD. Only when consistent efforts of the teacher fail to bring any significant improvement in the child's performance should the child be made to undergo screening and assessment procedures. Labelling a child with SLD at the slightest manifestation of any difficulty in language or arithmetic, pushing the child as 'special educator's child' and shirking off responsibility has been seen in many schools around. This needs to be reflected upon and the RTI, Response to Intervention has to be the road to genuine and dependable labelling a child as having SLD. Teacher and parents along with the help of counsellor can help a child by adopting flexible methodologies, assistive technology and encouraging positive attitudes towards self. Teachers who have a sound understanding of learning disabilities, child development and child psychology are better equipped to not only screen cases of SLD early, but also to work effectively along with special educators to design appropriate learning and assessment tasks for children with SLDs. Giving visual and auditory aids, using social stories and peer tutoring have been used successfully in the teaching-learning of children with SLD.

REFERENCES

Buonomo, I., Fiorilli, C., Geraci, M.A. and Pepe, A. (2017). "Temperament and Social-emotional difficulties: The dark side of learning disabilities", *The Journal of Genetic Psychology*, 1-14.

Cummins, A., Piek, J.P. and Dyck, M.J. (2005). "Motor coordination, empathy, and social behaviour in school-aged children". *Developmental Medicine and Child Neurology*, *47*(7): 437-442.

Harrison, M., Stockton, C. and Pearson, E. (2008, July). Inclusive, adaptive design for students with learning disabilities. In *Advanced Learning Technologies, 2008. ICALT'08. Eighth IEEE International Conference on* (pp. 1023-1027). IEEE.

Heward, W.L. (2009). *Exceptional Children: An Introduction to Special Education*. Pearson College Div.

Kundu, C.L. (2000). *Status of Disability in India—2000*. New Delhi: Rehabilitation Council of India, Ministry of Welfare, Government of India.

Lerner, J.W. and Kline, F. (2006). *Learning Disabilities and Related Disorders: Characteristics and Teaching Strategies*. Houghton Mifflin College Div.

Mangal, S.K. (2007). *Educating Exceptional Children: An Introduction to Special Education*, PHI Learning Pvt. Ltd.

Merbler, J.B., Hadadian, A. and Ulman, J. (1999). "Using assistive technology in the inclusive classroom". *Preventing School Failure: Alternative Education for Children and Youth*, *43*(3): 113-117.

Padhy, S.K. Goel, S., Das, S.S., Sarkar, S., and Sharma, V. (2015). "Prevalence and Patterns of Learning Disabilities in School Children", *The Indian Journal of Pediatrics* (2015): 1-7.

Quenneville, J. (2001). "Tech tools for students with learning disabilities: Infusion into inclusive classrooms", *Preventing School Failure: Alternative Education for Children and Youth*, *45*(4): 167-170.

Sale, P. and Carey, D.M. (1995). "The sociometric status of students with disabilities in a full-inclusion school". *Exceptional Children*, *62*(1): 6-19.

The Government of India (2010), The Right of Children to Free and Compulsory Education (RTE) Act 2009, Ministry of Human Resource Development, New Delhi: NCERT

Web Resources

Assistive Technology for Kids with Learning Disabilities: An Overview. (2017, September 06). Retrieved October 24, 2017, from http://www.readingrockets.org/article/assistive-technology-kids-learning-disabilities-overview

Cook, A. (n.d.). Peer Tutoring in Special Education. Retrieved October 23, 2017, from http://study.com/academy/lesson/peer-tutoring-in-special-education.html

Karanth P. (2002). Learning Disabilities in the Indian context, Available from: URL: http://.nalanda institute.org

Marc Dad and Developer (2014, May 07). Social Skills Deficits and Learning Disabilities: From a Teacher's Viewpoint. Retrieved on October 23, 2017 from http://thesocialexpress.com/social-skills-deficits-learning-disabilities-teachers-viewpoint /

Reid *et al.* (1994). http://drdineshsaroj.com/specific-learning-disability/

7

Visual Impairment and Inclusive Classrooms

Issues and Possibilities

Sangeeta Singh

Understanding Visual Impairment

Visual impairment is a generic term that includes a wide range of visual problems. It describes people who cannot see well even with correction. There are two main categories of visual impairment: one refers to people with low-vision and the other to those who are blind. The first category, comprising people with low vision, indicates that some functional vision exists which can be used for gaining information through written means with or without optical, non-optical or electronic devices. Children with low vision require some modifications to adapt in the regular school settings. On the other hand, children who are blind need major accommodations to be successful in regular schools.

Earlier, children with visual impairment (CwVI) were associated with lowered intellectual abilities, but in reality, the intellectual capabilities of students with visual impairment are similar to those of their sighted peers. However, significant academic delays have been shown by students with visual impairment due to their restricted ability to gain information visually. Unlike their sighted peers, CwVI have limited scope for incidental learning obtained from interaction with the environment. Therefore, conceptual development and learning experiences of CwVI predominantly depend on tactile experiences and the use of sensory modalities other than vision.

Visual impairment includes a reduction of visual acuity of near or distant vision or a restriction in the visual field. Acuity affects how well a child sees materials presented up close or work presented on blackboards or maps across the classroom. A child having impairment in the visual field may exhibit unusual head turnings and positioning in order to view the material with the fraction of visual field which is functional.

According to the Rights to Persons with Disabilities Act 2016, visual impairment includes two categories: Blindness and low vision.

a. "Blindness" stands for a condition where a person may have any of the following problems, after best correction:
   i) Total absence of sight; or
   ii) Visual acuity less than 3/60 or less than 10/200 (Snellen) in the better eye with best possible correction; or
   iii) Limitation of the field of vision subtending an angle of less than 10 degrees.
b. "Low vision" refers to a condition where a person has any of the following problems, namely:
   i) Visual acuity not exceeding 6/18 or less than 20/60 up to 3/60 or up to 10/200 (Snellen) in the better eye with best possible corrections; or
   ii) Limitation of the field of vision subtending an angle of less than 40 degrees up to 10 degrees.

> Visual acuity is measured by testing the smallest symbol that can be recognised. For example: 6/18, 6/60, 3/60. Here, the first number is the distance used for testing. Usually, this is 6, 3 or 1 metre. The second number is the size of the symbol read. The larger the second number, the larger the size of the symbol thus the worse vision.
>
> The sizes 60 and 18 are the distances in metres at which the shapes can be read by a person with normal vision. For example the symbol '24' could be read at 24 metres by someone with normal vision.

Kinds of Eye Ailments

1.	Nearsighted	The person cannot see things far away. The eye is too long, so the image does not reach the retina. This can be corrected by glasses
2.	Farsighted	The person cannot see things close up. The eye is too short, so the image falls behind the retina. This can be corrected by glasses.
3.	Astigmatism	It occurs when the cornea or lens is irregularly shaped which causes blurred vision. It can be corrected by glasses.
4.	Crossed Eyes (Strabismus)	It is a condition when a person's eyes are not able to align on the same point at the same time, and appear to be misaligned or pointed in different directions. This can be corrected by surgery, or by putting a patch over the good eye so that bad eye has to work.

(*Contd.*)

5.	Colour Blindness	Colour blindness occurs when a person is unable to see colours in a normal way. It can occur when one or more colour cone cells are absent, nonfunctioning, or detect a different colour than normal. This cannot be corrected.
6.	Night Blindness	It is also called Nyctalopia. Night blindness is due to a disorder of the cells
		in the retina that are responsible for vision in dim light.
7.	Optic Nerve Atrophy	Optic Nerve Atrophy (ONA) is degeneration of or damage to the optic nerve which carries vision information from the eye to the brain. Causes of ONA include heredity, trauma (including stroke), a tumor, decrease in oxygen or blood supply, infections, or disorders. The effects of ONA have a broad range dependending on the adequacy of visual messages sent from the eyes to the brain, from little or no visual impairment to near-total blindness. The condition may affect one or both eyes.
8.	Cataract	A cataract is an eye disease in which the clear lens of the eye becomes cloudy or opaque, causing a decrease in vision. It can be corrected through surgery.
9.	Glaucoma	Glaucoma is a disease that damages the eye's optic nerve. It usually happens when fluid builds up in the front part of the eye. That extra fluid increases the pressure in the eye thereby damaging the optic nerve.
10.	Detached Retina	Retinal detachment separates retinal cells from the layer of blood vessels that provides oxygen and nourishment. The longer the retinal detachment goes untreated, the greater the risk of permanent loss of vision in the affected eye.

Characteristics of Children with Visual Impairment (CwVI)

CwVI are a heterogeneous group. Similar to their sighted peers, every child with visual impairment has unique and individual characteristics. They differ in intellectual ability, rate of developmental, social competence and other factors. A common characteristic among them is that they have limited vision which impedes their ability to process information visually. The extent of their ability to process information visually becomes the critical factor which determines their success in education. However, within this overarching common characteristic, there are differences. They differ in the nature of their visual impairment, the extent of their visual capability, and their ability to use whatever vision they have. Some children have clear vision with significant field losses. Examples of restricted filed losses are given in Fig 1. Other CwVI may have significantly diminished visual acuities or blurred vision, which feels as if they are looking through a waxed paper and have full fields of vision. Their personalities, motivation, cognitive abilities and the extent to which they have learnt to use their residual vision vary. All these have strong educational implications.

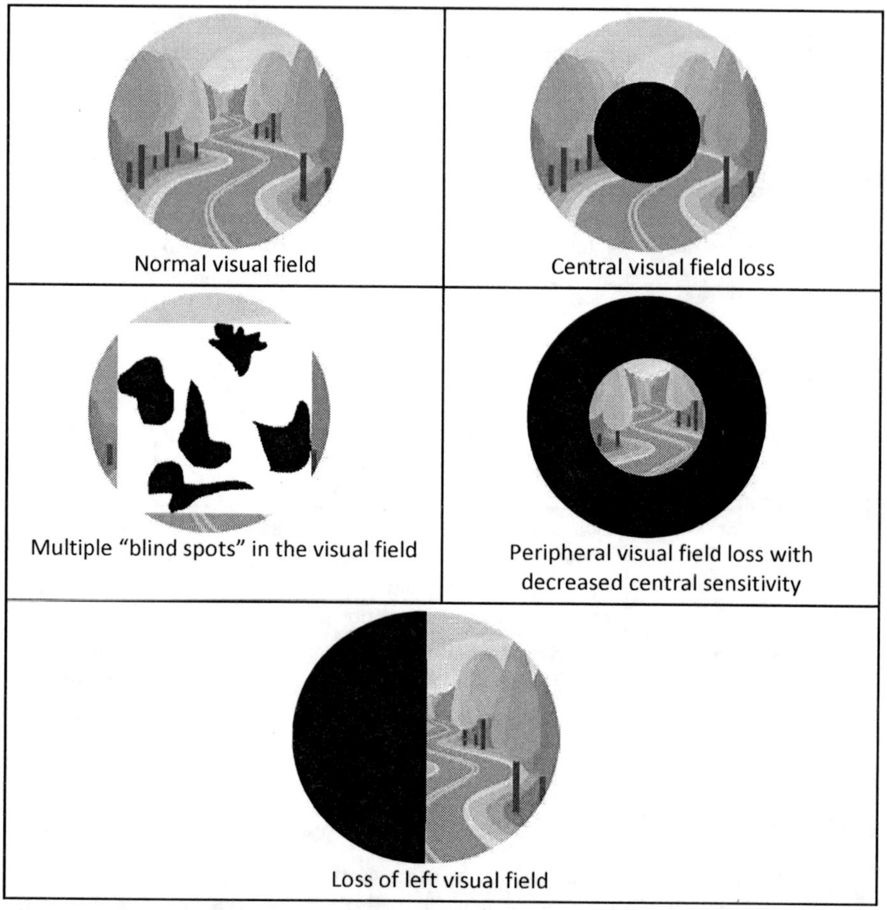

Fig. 7.1: Examples of restricted visual fields

Besides academics, limited vision impacts the psychological, communicative and socio-emotional aspects of the child's development. The degree of visual impairment, type of eye condition, age of the onset of problem, age of the student, gender, opportunities for movement and other experiences affect the academic needs, travelling skills, communication skills and vocational skills of the CwVI. Individuals identified as blind use tactile and auditory abilities as the primary medium of learning. Braille or other tactile media are commonly the preferred literacy channel. The primary channel of learning for children with low vision is through visual means with the use of prescription and nonprescription devices (for example, lenses, magnifying glasses and spectacles).

CwVI face challenges in their day-to-day life activities because they do not respond visually to people in their environment. Social behaviours which are taken for granted as learnt incidentally at a very young age by sighted people are difficult to learn for CwVI. Most of the social learning is accomplished through vision. Thus, visual impairment is a serious limitation for developing social skills and behaviour. For CwVI, skills such as eating skills, age-appropriate behaviour, clothing, knowledge about body parts and other social skills are not learned by observing people of their family and community. Therefore, CwVI must be taught these social skills purposefully.

Behavioural Manifestations

CwVI can be easily identified if their visual loss is severe. However, children with milder loss might pass several years without being recognised. Therefore,

Behaviour

- Rubs eyes excessively
- Shuts or covers one eye, tilts head, or thrusts head forward
- Has difficulty in reading or in other work requiring close use of eyes
- Blinks more than usual or is irritable when doing close work
- Holds books close to eyes
- Is unable to see distant things clearly
- Squints eyelids together or frowns

Appearance

- Crossed eyes
- Red-rimmed, encrusted, or swollen eyelids
- Inflamed or watery eyes
- Recurring sties in eyes

Complaints

- Itching, burning, or scratchy eyes
- Cannot see well
- Dizziness, headaches, or nausea following close eye work
- Blurred or double vision

Source: Exceptional Learners: Introduction to Special Education (9th ed., p. 343), by D.P. Hallahan and J. M. Kauffman, 2003. Boston: Allyn & Bacon.

teachers must be aware about the behaviours of children that are indicative of problem(s) in vision. However, some physical manifestations that appear to be symptomatic of visual impairment in children might be temporary. For example, a child may rub his/her eyes because of temporary eye infection or certain allergic reaction. Therefore, it is necessary to take cognisance of reasons for certain behaviours manifested by children before diagnosing them as visually impaired.

Inclusion of Children with Visual Impairment in Regular Classrooms

Usually, CwVI are not included in regular classrooms unless they are provided access to social and educational interventions. They need devices and technological support to fulfill their needs related to access to educational materials, visual presentations through auditory instructions, demonstrations and other activities along with regular teaching happening in the classroom. Apart from that, it is essential to raise awareness among sighted peers about their peers with visual impairment. For their successful inclusion in regular schools, CwVI must be accepted by teachers, staff members and sighted peers. It is important to highlight here that the educational goals for CwVI are effectively the same as those for sighted peers. These goals are effective communication, social competence, employability and personal independence. In order to achieve these goals, CwVI require specific interventions and modifications for educational programmes.

Role of Teachers

Role of teachers in addressing the needs of CwVI are multifaceted and they are expected to have knowledge across various disciplines in order to successfully facilitate inclusion of CwVI in regular classroom. Some such areas of knowledge include an understanding of:

- Medical conditions and diseases of eyes
- Types of magnification devices and assistive devices
- Educational and social needs of CwVI
- Schemes and Acts regarding the education of students with visual impairments
- Agencies and organisations working for CwVI
- Resources available for teaching academic content and social skills to CwVI.

Teachers must coordinate and consult other teachers, educational service providers and personnel who are working with CwVI to learn about ways of making educational programmes accessible and useful to them. It includes counsellor, educational psychologist, special educators, parents of children, social workers and personnel employed in organisations which work specially for CwVI.

CwVI need specific teaching strategies, modifications and interventions in the classroom. In addition to that, academic curriculum must be modified to meet the individual needs of each student so that progress is based on the level of skill(s) achieved and successful completion of expectations in each subject area. This section discusses the specific requirements of CwVI who thrive on their successful inclusion in the regular classroom.

Physical Education adaptations for children with visual impairments

Children with visual impairments need to be actively involved in physical education which helps them to develop necessary life skills and to maintain good health. CwVI can participate fully during physical education period with their sighted peers with certain adaptations and accommodations as suggested below:

- Use of beeping balls or rice in volley ball as an auditory accommodation
- Use of coloured balls or those that offer a high contrast to their surroundings for children with low vision
- Use of guide wire system or rope that is securely anchored to an eyehook or attached to poles to promote independence and encourage running. A PVC tube can be attached to the rope/wire so that the student can hold the tube and run along the rope.
- Provision of ropes, ground rail and special markers to help children move around the playground without difficulty.
- In learning a game, CwVI may be unable to imitate their peers' actions. Therefore, teachers may have to physically guide children's movement when introducing a physical activity.

Classroom Environment

The physical layout of the classroom is a major consideration in providing inclusive educational opportunities to students with VI. These students must be provided with such a classroom environment which enhances their access to educational materials and content taught in the classroom.

- Acquaint CwVI with the classroom and the school building by taking them around the spaces. Help them notice features such as location of desks, tables, doorways, stairs and materials. A clock orientation approach is useful for this purpose.

- Re-orient CwVI if the classroom arrangement is changed.
- Seat the CwVI in front of the classroom or close to the presentation area where they can hear the instructions clearly and correctly.
- Keep the furniture in fixed position. Inform CwVI if you rearrange the furniture while leaving classrooms.
- Keep the doors opened or closed and not partly open.
- Mark the glass doors well.
- Make sure that the walkways are not obstructed.
- People with visual impairment often rely on contrast to negotiate obstacles. Highlighting steps with a contrasting strip makes it easier for them to see the steps.
- Seat CwVI at a position where the lighting and glare from reflected surfaces does not distract their attention.
- Ensure proper lighting in classrooms
- Create extra space for CwVI so that they can use assistive devices such as note taker, portable magnifiers, etc. comfortably.

Points to be kept in mind during classroom transaction

- Address all students by their names so that CwVI can recognise them by their voices.
- Use verbal explanations while using audio-visual aids, presentations and demonstrations for teaching content.
- Speak out whatever you write on the blackboard.
- Take breaks at regular intervals to minimise the fatigue in listening or using Braille by the CwVI.
- Eliminate auditory distractions.
- Identify yourself by name, in case the CwVI does not recognise you by your voice.
- Indicate verbally when you entre or leave the classroom.
- Try to stay in the same place and not move around while you are talking.

Teaching Strategies

- During group discussions, ensure that only one person speaks at a time so that the CwVI can easily follow the thread of the conversation.
- While teaching through presentations, provide reading material and slides in advance to prevent exclusion and reducing delay.
- While organising field trips and excursions, inform the staff members at sites in advance about the participation of student(s) with visual impairment. It would help them make necessary arrangements/

adaptations for students with VI to facilitate their participation in various activities during the trip.

- CwVI are not aware of the messages displayed on notice boards or written on whiteboards. Therefore, ensure that there are verbal announcements of notices.
- While teaching new terms, give oral explanation and spell the word so that CwVI can comprehend the meaning of new terms.
- State orally the steps and procedures involved in carrying out mathematical calculations.
- Provide alternative time with an assistant, who can be a sighted peer, if necessary, to view the videos shown at classes on regular basis.

Socio-emotional Interventions

- Encourage CwVI to participate in co-curricular activities and make use of leadership opportunities provided by the institution.
- Be patient. Observe the child silently and encourage him to do her/his work independently. Provide minimal assistance only if it is required by the child to build up self-confidence and foster independence.
- Reinforce them for their every effort and the smallest of achievements.
- Encourage CwVI to be advocates for them. Create activities in which they have to make decisions and choices that will have an impact on the outcome of the activity for all the students.
- Encourage CwVI to share their expertise in specific activities with the class. For example, let the CwVI demonstrate the use of Braille note taker.
- During physical education or other non-academic activities, teach games that will allow all students, including CwVI, to participate actively and promote group cooperation.

Peer Mediated Interventions and Support Network

Peers provide a natural way for CwVI to learn social skills. Teachers can select some sighted students for peer intervention who can demonstrate various social skills. Under the direction of teachers, these peers can receive instructions on how to target selected social skills to train the CwVI. Technically, selected peers may not have expertise in teaching strategies, but peer support and feedback motivate CwVI to learn a variety of social skills.

Sighted peers are expected to learn about the etiology of the students' ophthalmic ailment, how CwVI function in the school and community, and assistive devices and equipment used by them.

Peer support network is a strategy that can be used in regular classrooms to assist CwVI wherein sighted peers are assigned explicit roles in assisting students with VI. For example, sighted peers are encouraged to:

- Support CwVI in setting up and keeping track of their equipment and special devices
- Support CwVI in reading information from the blackboard or overhead projectors, cueing the student to raise his/her hand and alerting the student with VI about non-verbal actions or activities taking place in the classroom.
- Assist CwVI with activities during recess by including them in games and activities on the playground.

(The above tasks can be taken up by sighted students in rotation so that the entire peer group gets sensitised.)

A Message from Blind People

(*Read it with utmost attention*)

1. I'm an ordinary person, just blind. You don't need to raise your voice or address me as if I were a child. Don't ask my companion what I want, just ask me directly. Always remember that I just cannot see but I can hear clearly. Talk to me so that we will understand each other better.
2. If I am walking with you, don't grab my arms, let me take yours. I'll keep a half step behind to anticipate curbs and steps. Don't be overcautious and make a full stop at every step. Walk normally and your body movement will tell me what to do.
3. When you see me walking alone down the hall, don't hesitate to offer assistance. Just tap slightly on the shoulder and say, excuse me or hello to call my attention. Don't whisper behind my back. I'm not some alien from outer space to be laughed at or frightened of.
4. I want to know who's in the room with me, speak when you enter. It is helpful to mention your name or say hello each time we meet, especially for new acquaintances, so that the sound of your voice will be familiar and recognisable to me. Introduce me to the others including children, and tell me if there's a cat or a dog. Guide my hand to a chair by letting me touch the backrest.
5. The door to a room, cabinet or a car left partially open is a hazard to me. Make a habit to leave doors or rooms or cabinet drawers fully opened or closed.

   I also need a sense of permanence in the room or in the drawer. Classroom fixtures must have their designated places so that I can memorise the place.

   Don't leave chairs or bags in the middle of the room because I might trip over it. Kindly draw your curtains such that they don't hinder when I enter your room.

6. At meal times, I will not have trouble with ordinary table skills. Use the clock method when describing to me the food on my plate or the position of my glass of water or cup of coffee. For example, 12:00 to tell that my viand is at the uppermost centre of my plate, 11:00 if my glass of water is at the upper left side, etc.
7. Don't avoid words like see, I use it too. I'm always glad to see you. My sense of smell, touch or hearing did not improve when I became blind. I rely on them more and, therefore, may get more information through those senses than you do. That's all!
8. If I'm your house guest, show me the bathroom, closet, dresser, windows and the light switch too. I like to know whether the lights are on.
9. I'll discuss blindness with you if you are curious, but it's an old story to me. I have as many interests as you do. However, don't be afraid to ask questions. We blind people are more than willing to explain to you all that you wish to know. It's better to clarify things you don't understand than make hasty assumptions. Remember, questions don't hurt, ignorance does.
10. Please make me a part of your world. I also enjoy the same things you do. Parties, movies, school competitions. Let me participate in these activities, and you'll be surprised that I can be as fun as the person next to you.
11. Don't think of me as just a blind person. I'm just a person who happens to be blind.

Source: Written by an activist group of Blind people in Delhi.

Use of Assistive Devices

Assistive technology refers to a range of tools, devices, and strategies that allow a student to accomplish a task that they would otherwise be unable to do, or would have difficulty accomplishing effectively. Assistive technology can be simple or complex. The primary purpose of assistive devices and technologies is to maintain or improve the functioning of people, to foster independence in them and facilitate participation to enhance their overall well-being.

Children with VI have a broad range of visual abilities and needs. Every child with VI is unique and has specific requirements that may not be present in other children. Therefore, it is essential to consider the views of family members, educators, service providers and the student with VI while selecting assistive technology for her/him. Some of the assistive devices that can be used by children with VI are:

1. *Walking Canes*: Canes for the blind and visually impaired are one of the most important identification and mobility aids for people who are either blind or have low vision. It helps them gain independence and freedom while travelling.

2. *Screen Readers*: It is a type of software which is also known as text-to-speech application. The software analyses the characters, words and sentences, and converts them into digital speech. For Example, JAWS (Job Access with Speech) is the world's most popular screen reader, developed for computer users with visual impairments. JAWS provides speech and Braille output for the most popular computer applications on the PC.
3. *Braille Technology:* With the advent of technology, access to educational materials in Braille has become easy. There are various kinds of devices related to Braille, such as Braille display, Braille embosser, Braille translation software and Braille note taker.

   Braille display: A braille display device operates by lowering and raising different combinations of pins electronically to produce in braille what appears on a portion of the computer screen.

   Braille embosser: The braille embosser is a printer attached to a computer which is used to produce a braille copy of text. A braille embosser may also be attached to braille note taking devices for the same purpose.

   Braille translation software: Braille translation software converts printed text into braille. Translated text may then be printed for the student using a Braille embosser (Braille printer).

   Braille note taker: Electronic braille note taking devices may be used by a student to take notes in class using either a Braille or standard (QWERTY) keyboard. Those notes may then be transferred to a computer for storage, or printed in either braille or print formats. Many note taking devices have word processors, appointment calendars, calculators or clocks and can perform functions similar to a computer. Some note taking devices have a speech programme with braille input and some also feature a refreshable braille display.

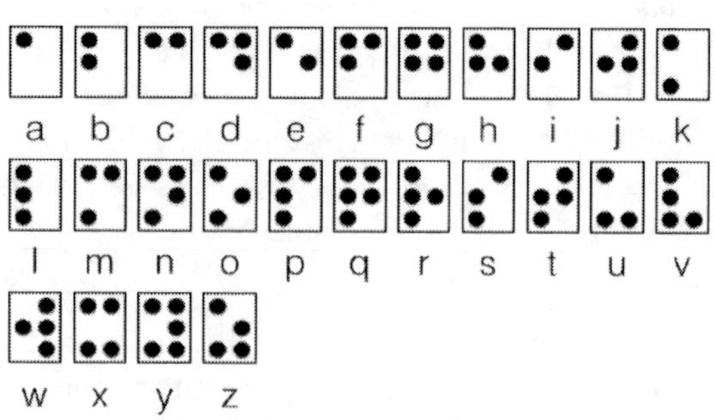

Fig. 7.2: English Alphabets in Braille.

Source: https://www.royalblind.org

4. *Large type keyboard*: It is useful for children with low vision while typing on the keyboard.
5. *Magnifiers:* There is a wide range of magnifiers including mouse magnifiers, desktop magnifiers, video magnifiers, handheld magnifiers, portable magnifiers and computer screen magnifiers available for people with low vision to make the content readable as per their need.

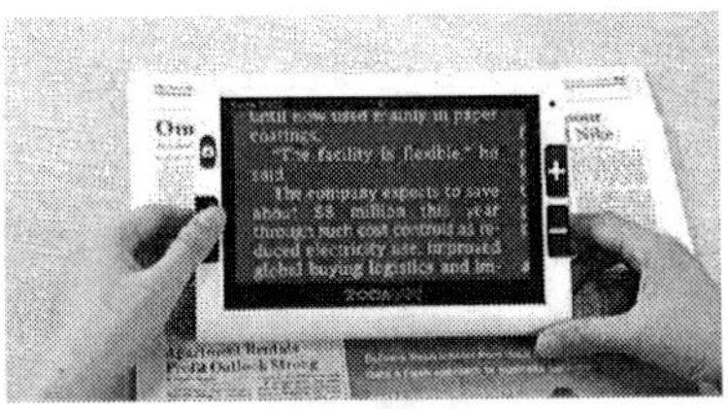

Hand held Magnifier

Video Magnifier

Computer screen magnifiers: Computer magnification software can be used to view digital text. It can be customised by magnification level, area of display being magnified and visual qualities of display.

Video magnifiers: A video magnifier, or closed-circuit television (CCTV), provides a magnified image for use by people with low vision to enable them to maintain an independent lifestyle at work, home, or school. A video magnifier consists of a camera, monitor, lighting, and usually a stand. In addition to providing magnification, video magnifiers usually have enhanced contrast and other features that help to read magazines and letters, view family photos, write checks, do school related work and other activities.

Handheld magnifiers: Handheld magnifiers are useful for children with low vision for reading labels on medicine bottles or strips, restaurant menus, bus/train time schedule chart and text given in books, magazines and newspapers.

6. *Talking devices*: Talking devices are used by people with visual impairment to gain information in auditory form. There are several devices, such as Talking colour recogniser, Talking wrist watches, Talking calculators, Talking weighing machine, Talking blood pressure machine and Talking keyboards available in India.
7. *Touch memo*: It is a labeling tool that identifies every object without any difficulty. Touch Memo is a digital voice labeler that is about the size of a pen that records and plays message when it touches a supplied label.
8. *DAISY reader and recorder*: DAISY stands for Digital Accessible Information System. It is a digital book format that offers many

advantages over traditional audio books on a traditional audio CD. DAISY books may contain both text and sound. It can be read on a portable digital playback device, a regular mp3 player or on a computer equipped with playback software.

There are certain DAISY audio players which have a built-in speech synthesiser that reads documents aloud from a variety of sources, such as word processor and internet. They can also play audio books, music files and access DAISY books.

HV Player

Plex Talk Vachak

DAISY Player and Recorder

Visual impairment is a low incidence disability that does not affect a large number of children within school. Historically, CwVI were associated with intellectual disabilities. Though they do lag behind their sighted peers in academics and social development, it is incorrect to relate it with intellectual disabilities. Limited vision restricts their educational, social and physical development. However, with curricular adaptations, special teaching strategies and accommodations in classrooms and physical activities, CwVI can perform at par with their sighted peers. Educators need to make efforts to understand the needs of CwVI, design a variety of teaching materials, and use suitable resources for their proper inclusion. Further, the advancement in technology has enabled CwVI to participate in schools and communities along with their sighted peers. Working with CwVI requires knowledge of specific methods, orientation mobility training, the Braille system and use of various objects and tactile materials.

Conclusion

Visual impairment is a low incidence disability as we do not see many children with this disability in our regular schools, the reason for this being many. Historically, CwVI were looked upon to be having intellectual disabilities. Though they do lag behind their sighted peers in academics and social development, it is incorrect to relate it with intellectual disabilities. Limited vision restricts their educational, social and physical development. However, with curricular adaptations, special teaching strategies and accommodations in classrooms and physical activities, CwVI can perform at par with their sighted peers. Educators need to make efforts to understand the needs of CwVI, design and use the necessary range of learning materials and other suitable resources for their successful inclusion. Further, the advancement in technology has enabled CwVI to participate in schools and communities along with their sighted peers. Working with CwVI requires knowledge of specific methods, orientation mobility training, the braille system and use of various objects and tactile materials. Above all positive attitude and confidence from people around are vital for the functioning and participation of CwVI in any environment.

REFERENCES

Sacks, S.Z. and Wolffe, K.E. (2006). *Teaching Social Skills to Students with Visual Impairment: From Theory to Practice*. New York: AFB Press, American Foundation for the Blind.

Mangal, S.K. (2009). *Educating Exceptional Children: An Introduction to Special Education.* New Delhi: PHI Learning Private Limited.

Smith, T.E., Polloway, E.A., Doughty, T.T., Patton, J.R. and Dowdy, C.A. (2013). *Teaching students with Special Needs in Inclusive Settings*, Delhi: PHI Learning Private Limited.

Gargiulo, R.M. (2015). *Special education in contemporary society: An Introduction to exceptionality*. (5th Ed.), LA: SAGE.

Roe, J. and Webster, A. (2002). *Children with Visual Impairments: Social Interaction, Language and Learning.* London: Routledge.

Saracho, O.N. (2012). *An Integrated play-based curriculum for young children*. New York: Routledge.

Bayat, M. (2017). Teaching exceptional children: Foundations and best practices, *Inclusive Early Childhood Education Classrooms*. New York: Routledge.

Cook, R.E., Richardson-Gibbs, A.M., Nielsen, L., and Klein, M.D. (2018). *Strategies for including children with special needs in early childhood settings*. Boston, MA, USA: Cengage Learning.

Web Resources

https://nfb.org/ https://www.afb.org/

http://www.medindia.net/health_statistics/general/visualimpairment.asp

http://www.lowvisiononline.unimelb.edu.au/Screening/acuity.htm

http://www.teachingvisuallyimpaired.com/pe-adaptations.html

http://www.bpaindia.org/pdf/VIB%20Chapter-VII.pdf

http://www.cbmindia.org.in/article/downloads/136867/Directory_of_Assistive_Devices.pdf

http://www.rsvi.org/rsvi-aids-appliances.php

https://www.royalblind.org

8

Teacher Education within the Ambit of Disability and Inclusion

A Reflection

Alka Behari

In order to understand the implications for teacher preparation in a proper perspective, it becomes important to reiterate some aspects related to inclusion discussed earlier in this book.

The concept of inclusion places the emphasis on changing the system rather than the child. Proponents of inclusion insist that it is *not* necessary for a student with disabilities to be "at grade level" in order to receive instruction in the general education setting. The argument is that our educational system, structure and practices need to shift and become more flexible, more inclusive, and more collaborative in order to better accommodate students with learning differences. The primary assertion made is that it is a Human Right for all individuals to be included. This gets reinforced by the 'word' of Law, since, legally, according to the Individuals with Disabilities Education Act (IDEA); students with disabilities are to be educated in the 'least' restrictive environment. According to many professionals, parents, advocates and consumers, this means that the general classroom itself assumes great importance.

In this perspective, inclusive schooling is often thought of as the inclusion of all students, regardless of ability, into the same schools, and classrooms with peers who are not considered to have disabilities. However, as highlighted in the earlier sections, inclusive schooling extends far beyond mere physical proximity. It is potentially both a process and an outcome for achieving social justice and equity in our society

The above discussed background compels us to try and understand how we would prepare future teachers and educate those who are teachers at present, to be sensitive and inclusive with regard to students with disabilities.

Summarising the Need and Basis for Teacher Preparation in the Context of Learners with Disabilities

- There is a global shortage of teachers who are sufficiently trained and motivated to include children with disabilities in regular schools. Yet, such inclusion is vital for achieving Education for All goals and bringing the millions of currently excluded children into education.
- In order to develop skills, experience and confidence to be inclusive of all children, teachers need to learn and practise inclusive education during pre-service and in-service training, and they need to be given opportunities for continuing professional development (which extends beyond simply attending training courses) throughout their careers.
- Policy makers and trainers responsible for developing teacher training and for recruiting teachers need to understand inclusive education and its importance for educational improvement. The concept of inclusive education as a *twin-track* approach needs to be grasped, which can improve the quality of education for all, yet also provide specialised support, where needed, for children with disabilities.
- Every teacher needs to learn about inclusive education, from day one of his/her training. This should be achieved by embedding inclusion, rights and equality throughout all training and not simply covering these issues through stand-alone courses.
- Every teacher also needs opportunities for inclusive education practicum during training; and to feel supported (e.g. by specialist colleagues) to continue trying new ideas. There needs to be an effective balance of theoretical and practical learning for teachers at pre-service and in-service stages. Inclusive education training and continuous professional development need to be designed and given with inputs from diverse stakeholders—in particular, from the community and professionals with disabilities—to give a stronger sense of reality to teachers' learning experiences.
- Good practices need to be documented and shared in relation to training quality teachers for including children with disabilities.

A Peep into History

The international community has committed itself to achieving universal basic education through the Millennium Development Goals (MDG) and the Education for All goals. Yet these frameworks pay insufficient attention to marginalised groups such as children with disabilities—which is a major reason why they continue to miss out on quality education. However, the 2010 MDG report is the first one to focus on disabilities, along with the 2011 World Disability Report, and the State of the World's Children 2013 report—all focus on children with disabilities and the importance of inclusive education.

In India, inclusive education for children with disability has only recently been accepted in policy and in principle. Researchers now argue for individual initiative on the part of schools to implement programmes of inclusive education for children with mild to moderate disabilities in classrooms. Curriculum adaptations, teaching methodology and evaluation procedures can be adapted to suit the needs of children with disabilities. The National Curriculum Framework (NCF) 2005 document laid a special focus by bringing out the Position Paper on Children with Special Needs. More recently, the National Council of Teacher Education (NCTE) Regulations 2014 has laid special emphasis and included inclusive education as a core component of all teacher education programmes. As Florian and Rouse (2009) state—The task of initial teacher education is to prepare people to enter a profession which accepts individual and collective responsibility for improving the learning and participation of all children. And, according to Mckinsey et al (2009)—'the quality of an education system cannot exceed the quality of its teachers.'

Approaches for Teacher Preparation in the Context of Inclusion of Children with Disabilities

While we may not be able to highlight any universal way of preparing teachers, a broad framework may still be considered to discuss how teacher education can be structured. The following points have been taken from Reiser (2013):

1. Professional development of teachers needs to be seen as part of a whole system approach to change. This urges for induction and continuing professional development for teachers to make them aware of recent developments regarding inclusion of children with disabilities. The challenge is to convince teachers that they have a responsibility to uphold the education rights of *all* learners. The World Report on Disability (WHO, 2011) emphasises the need for teacher education on inclusion to be about attitudes and values, not just about knowledge and skills. This is a challenge since, *even for children with mild to moderate disabilities,* there has historically been segregated special education, relieving mainstream teachers of the responsibility of teaching many children.

Teacher Education has to be structured around inclusion that is integrated, embedded or permeated. Teaching separate courses would not help. Thus, inclusion is to be an integral part of the curriculum for all students of teacher education, rather than an optional add-on. This notion has to permeate all pre-service and in-services courses, distance learning programmes, informal discussions, mentoring systems and cluster school programmes (Stubbs, 2011).

2. School-based training, aimed at supporting school development would contribute in empowering future teachers. This is evident in several countries where student-teachers are taught the theory of inclusive education without any opportunities to practise and gain confidence with teaching methods to support diverse learners, including those with disabilities. A research study reveals that resource trainers acted as mentors to existing teachers in mainstream schools and there was much sharing of experience at the seminars organised. This helped teachers to tackle many challenges that they were facing. UNESCO's Policy Guidelines on Inclusion in Education (2009) supports the move to school-based teacher education and highlights the importance of a shift away from theoretical pre-service teacher education towards 'continuous in-service development of teachers.

3. Where training resources are scarce, cascade models can enable training to be disseminated throughout the system. In this model, 'a relatively small number of professionals' is trained, who then have to disseminate (or 'cascade') their skills and knowledge to wider groups, who in turn cascade to others.

4. Emphasis on Continuing Professional Development of Teachers—It is now well recognised that pre-service teacher education cannot prepare teachers for every challenge that they meet, and so teacher education needs to be perceived as a life-long process of professional development (Rouse, 2012). It is also being realised that many of the more successful approaches to educating teachers for inclusion are at the in-service stage, when teachers have some experiences of teaching, and have real life challenges and children to work with. A study reveals the case where teachers produced a collection of reflective accounts as they worked with children with disabilities. To be effective, in-service training needs to be continuous, reflective, interactive and well led by the principal / administrator of the school. (Rieser, 2013)

5. Supporting teachers to become collaborative reflective practitioners—According to Rieser, "teachers already have a lot of knowledge and need to learn how to make better use of it. What teachers lack is often confidence in their own competence when it comes to including children with disabilities. *Transformability* is a concept gaining ground, whereby teachers can transform learning for all pupils, with the pupils 'co-agency'—learning is, thus, the responsibility of both teacher and learner (Hart *et al.*, 2004). For this, teachers need to be educated as reflective practitioners who learn skills of collaboration and teamwork with other teachers, para-professionals and parents (Ainscow, 2004). Organising workshops for teachers can give them an insight into the variety of (non-formal) techniques that may be used for teaching / learning.

Implications for the Curriculum of Pre-service Teacher Education

The increasing demands within the educational environment have implications for the curriculum for teacher trainers / student – teachers. UNESCO's Policy Guidelines on inclusion in education mention the need for future teachers to be trained in teamwork, skills for working with parents and civil society, ability to adapt to different age groups, interactive methods, ability to respond to gender and the individual needs of all learners.

Forgac's meta-review of pre-service teacher education highlights the problem with inclusion not being an over-arching concept within teacher education curricula in schools (Forgac, 2012). This gap needs to be addressed.

It is vital for the school system to be convinced that working with children of all abilities is the responsibility of everybody, not just specialists (Blanton & Pugach, 2007; Florian & Rouse, 2009).

Florian and Rouse (2009) propose that teachers should be encouraged to view inclusion as an approach for all, rather than being specialist, different or unusual.

Some Skills / Knowledge/Competencies that need to be developed among all student-teachers are:

- planning and teaching for inclusion
- awareness of the emotional and mental health of needs of pupils (to build their self-esteem as learners)
- assessment for learning (learning skills)
- an understanding of the following —
  - Difference is a normal aspect of development
  - Teachers are capable of teaching all children
  - Teachers must develop collaborative ways of working.

Implications for Pedagogy

There are two main issues in relation to pedagogy of inclusion:

- The pedagogy that teachers use in the classroom
- The pedagogy that is used during the teacher education programme.

The two are inter-linked. Several university teacher educators have limited experience of working with these approaches (Forgac, 2012). Pedagogy is crucial to pre-service teachers and in-service teachers. In addition to the skills listed in the previous section, other methods may also be discussed. Mitchell (2008) analyses the various pedagogy and methods that have proved effective for learners with special needs. Some of these are—cooperative group teaching, peer training, social skills training, self-regulation learning, direct instruction, review and practice, formative assessment and feedback, and assistive technology.

Most of these strategies have been found to be effective for all learners. Therefore, such methods ought to be taught to teachers / student teachers. Perner & Porter (2008) present ways of approaching learners, including children with disabilities, from a whole-class teaching pedagogy. They assert that teachers require thorough pre-service and ongoing in-service training to ensure the success of whole-class pedagogy. Essential skills include adapting curricula, using a variety of instructional strategies, collaborating and solving problems, developing individualised instruction plans, and monitoring student progress. Perner & Porter, further, talk of an Innovative Pedagogy: Multilevel Instruction. They define this approach to classroom instruction and organisation that provides students with varying levels of academic skills and appropriate opportunities through the same core lesson. Continuing further, it is seen that, in this context, Davis & Florian (2004) establish the point there is no separate pedagogy for children with disabilities that is just exclusive for them. Let us try to understand this deeper. At the outset, it needs to be stated that this assertion is, in no way, antithetical to what Perner & Porter have said. Rather, it may be considered to offer an explanation of the underlying theoretical basis of the whole-class teaching pedagogy approach. According to Davis & Florian, although there is a great deal of literature that might be seen as 'special education knowledge', the teaching approach and strategies themselves are influenced by the same basic research. The term 'special education' is often used to refer to the process of making accommodations that does not constitute a separate pedagogy, but it is an element of the broad pedagogy itself. Thus, it may be concluded that there is a need for all teachers to develop a pedagogy that is inclusive of *all* learners.

The most challenging target of any teacher preparation curricula is improving attitudes of student-teachers. Several studies show that teachers' attitudes shape the promotion of inclusion (Forlin & Chambers, 2011), and that training is particularly important in developing positive attitudes and practices (Gwernan, Jones & Burden, 2010). Elhoweris & Alsheikh (2006) suggest that attitudes can be improved by increasing students' knowledge about learners with disabilities and ways to meet their learning needs. They suggest that teacher education programmes may need to include more alternative learning styles and instructional strategies. They propose the use of successful inclusive teachers and individuals with disabilities as guest teachers and the use of disability simulation in order to foster sensitivity and positive attitudes among future teachers. A further example comes from Cambodia. Here, in a teacher education programme, sessions were developed for pre-service student-teachers through which performance art was used to work with people with disabilities. This also raised the level of sensitivity among the student-teachers.

Inclusive pedagogies are in a state of evolution. Each student with disability paves ways of equipping the teacher with diverse teaching learning styles. Teachers learn many more pedagogies through their practice as compared to the 'official knowledge' attained through pre-service and in-service programmes. Acknowledging this fact, it is significant for a teacher to be open to observing and learning from each day's experience. It is even more important that teachers are trained to share and discuss their professional experiences through varied forums of teachers or through online forums to cover larger teacher groups.

Besides this, sharing of **success stories** of persons with disabilities during discussions in the classes, parents' narrations of rearing children with disabilities, field visits to NGOs working with disabilities, watching movies related to people with disabilities, videos on education of children with disabilities and their lives in general can all be effective learning strategies for prospective teachers.

Two success stories have been presented below.

Success Stories from the Satya Special School
(including a presentation of the Parents' Perspective National Centre for Learning Disabilities)

Case 1

Anuj is a five-year-old child with attention deficit hyperactivity disorder (ADHD). He was also diagnosed with delayed speech and language development and had poor pre linguistic skills, linguistic skills, and pragmatic skills. Paralinguistic skills: Lack of eye contact, attention and concentration, receptive skills and expressive skills, poor vocabulary levels and did not mingle with any of the peer groups. When Anuj first came to the Centre, he was always uncomfortable and wanted to leave the classroom; he used one word sentences that were not clear and expressed his needs through gestures and finger pointing.

After he attended the speech therapy session, we adopted a play method of teaching due to which Anuj started enjoying his sessions. Anuj's mother also co-operated very well. After six months of training, Anuj could speak two-three word sentences that fulfilled his needs. From one word, his vocabulary has increased to more than 100 words. He is now able to express the names of all animals and vehicles, etc. His pragmatic skills have also improved and he has now been integrated into a play school. The feedback from the play school teachers is very encouraging. They say that Anuj is communicating with others and doing a good job at school. Anuj's mother is very pleased with his progress and is optimistic about the future of her child.

Case 2

A year ago, when no school was willing to even admit my son, the team at Satya not only provided the necessary therapy but also encouraged both my wife and me to take life positively. From a state when he was only lying down for hours together, today he stands using the standing table. His eye contact has increased and he smiles when spoken to. I would have never believed that my son would one day sit with support but all this is becoming a reality today. Thanks to the dedication of the staff and the facilities in the centre. The centre is an answer to the hopes of parents of children with special needs like me"—*Suryanathan's father.*

Implications for Role, Place and Development of Teacher Educators

Classroom teachers are key individuals in successful inclusive practice. Providing the supportive environment for the students is one of the crucial tasks of any teacher. This can be easily situated within the tenets of disability theory, in particular the social model of disability which 'rejects the emphasis of individual impairment in favour of a focus on the disabling aspects of the environment, including culture, attitudes and institutions' (Oliver, 2013). Therefore, shifting the focus from the impairment of the learners as a problem, teachers need to provide tailored transactional strategies and psycho-socially conducive environment to nurture the learner and enable learning.

Teachers often have positive attitudes and are sympathetic towards learners with diverse needs; but many do not see themselves as having the skills, experience or resources to effectively support these learners (De Boer, Pijl, & Minnaert, 2011; MacFarlane & Woolfson, 2013).

What do teacher educators need to be equipped with in order to understand inclusive education? They need to have a 'sound' understanding of inclusive education as an approach and philosophy that underpins educational improvement. They need to understand that there are certain practices that generally support all learners, including children with disabilities, but there are skills required to meet the specific learning needs of students with disabilities as well. Needless to say, these pupil teachers' conviction that children with mild to moderate levels of disabilities can be effectively included in the classroom processes is inevitable.

An inclusive classroom is where varied strategies that enable learning for all students are tried out and implemented on a long term basis. It is seen that centres of education are trying to provide accessibility and promote the use of assistive aids to enable learning. The concept of enabling accessibility is somehow thought useful to persons with visible disabilities (Braille, sign language, JAWS software, etc.), whereas there is resistance to accommodate learners with softer disabilities or not so obvious disabilities such as autism, dyslexia, etc.

With learners with not so obvious disability in the inclusive classroom, teachers have to look beyond the invisibility of the condition and remind themselves that the student indeed *has* disability with its associated needs, despite appearing as any other student in the peer group and not manifesting any 'visible signs' of their condition. Teachers have to search deeply into their understanding of the disability to try out and implement alternative strategies to infer the behaviour and needs of children with disability in order to facilitate effective learning.

Teacher educators not only have the role of supporting student-teachers' learning about teaching but they also model the role of the teacher. Korthagen et al (2005) said—The way teacher educators model the promotion of certain views of learning could be a more important factor in shaping teacher behaviour than the content of what they teach.

According to Grimes (2009), teacher educators not only need 'training' but also the same classroom experiences and observations of approaches as their teacher trainees. Exposing them to ***best practices*** also contributes in their development. They need to have critical self – awareness and be models of reflective inclusive practice themselves. Co-teaching or collaboration between teacher educators is also seen to facilitate their teaching. Boling (2007) suggests that teacher educators should use *case methodology* to encourage student-teachers to reflect upon and possibly change their fixed notions, beliefs and prior assumptions. This would enable the student-teachers to cater to the needs of students with disabilities when they enter the world of teaching.

Inclusive education can become a reality only if the teachers involved are convinced about and committed to inclusive education. The success of inclusive education derives from multiple factors. But no matter how well articulated an educational policy, however excellent the educational infrastructure, or how well resourced a programme might be, effective inclusion does not take place until regular classroom teachers deliver relevant and meaningful instruction to students with disabilities (Mastropieri & Scruggs, 2010). Roles played by teachers in inclusive classes are varied. They mentor and nurture the students thus setting the conducive tone and warm ethos of the classes. They become role models, remain vigilant, observant, keep their ears and eyes open to listen and look for signs of trouble, and diffuse and resolve challenges. All these roles can be successfully played only when they are professionally satisfied and enjoy a sense of fulfilment in their daily practice. If teaching is perceived merely as a task to be completed by a teacher, inclusion will remain a far-flung delusion. It is critical that the teacher is invested in inclusion.

Conclusion

The following principles have emerged as key ingredients for effective teacher-education, keeping in view the need of inclusive education of children with disabilities:

- Inclusive education needs to be a comprehensive strategy central to all teacher education.
- Giving all teachers grounding in inclusion and disability studies would develop a strong empathy among them.
- Teacher educators need to be conversant with the recent paradigm shift to a social / human rights approach, challenging medically and psychologically based approaches which view children with disabilities as a deficit. They need to model inclusion themselves in their approach and practices.
- Future teachers need to be trained as reflective practitioners, problem solvers, collaborative workers and action researchers.
- 'Special' education teachers can play the role of Resource Persons in mainstream schools. Teachers, with their assistance, can be trained to set up Resource Centres at their schools to make materials readily available for teaching all learners, including those with disabilities.

REFERENCES

Ainscow, M. (2004). Special Needs in the Classroom: A teacher education guide. Paris: UNESCO.

Boling, E. (2007). "Yeah, but I still don't want to deal with it". Changes in a Teacher Candidate's Conceptions of Inclusion". *Teaching Education*, 18 (3), September 2007. 217-231

Davis, P and Floran, L. (2004). "*Teaching strategies and approaches for pupils with special educational needs: A scoping study*." Department for Education and Skills: Research Report No. 516. http://www.education.gov.uk

De Boer, A., Pijl, S.J. and Minnaert, A. (2011). "Regular primary schoolteachers' attitudes towards inclusive education: A review of the literature". *International journal of inclusive education*, 15, 331-353.

Ethoweris, H. and Alsheikh, N. (2006). "*Teachers' Attitudes Towards Inclusion*", *International Journal of Special Education*, 21(1): 115-118.

Forlin, C. and Chambers, D. (2011). "Teacher preparation for inclusive education: Increasing knowledge but raising concerns", *Asia-Pacific Journal of Teacher Education*, 39, 17-32.

Florian, L. and Rouse, M. (2009). "The Inclusive Practice Project in Scotland: Teacher Education for Inclusive Education", *Teaching and Teacher Education*, 25: 594-601.

Forgacs, R.T. (2012). 'Strengthening Teacher Education to Achieve EFA by 2015: How are student-teachers prepared to adopt inclusive attitudes and practices when they start teaching?' Consultancy Report, UNESCO

Gwernan-Jones, R. and Burden, R.L. (2010). "Are they just lazy? Student teachers' attitudes about dyslexia". *Dyslexia, 16*, 66-86.

Hart, S. Dixon, A., Drummond, M.J. Mcintyre, D. (2004). *Learning without Limits*. Milton Keynes: Open University.

Korthagen, F., Loughran, J., Lumenberg, M. (2005). 'Teaching teachers: Studies into the expertise of teacher educators'. *Teaching and Teacher Education*, 21 (2): 107-115

MacFarlane, K. and Woolfson, L.M. (2013). "Teacher attitudes and behaviour toward the inclusion of children with social, emotional and behavioural difficulties in mainstream schools: an application of the theory of planned behaviour", *Teaching and teacher education*, *29*, 46-52.

Mastropieri M.A. and Scruggs T.E. (2010). *Inclusive classroom: The Strategies for effective instruction*, Pearson: NY.

McKinsey and Co. (2007). *How the world's best performing school systems come out on top*. Available online at: http://www.mckinsey.com/locations/UK

Mitchell, D. (2008). What really works in special and inclusive education: Using evidence based teaching strategies. London: Routledge

NCF (2005). National Focus Group Position Paper—Education of Children with Special Needs, New Delhi: NCERT.

NCTE (2014). *NCTE Regulations*. New Delhi: National Council for Teacher Education (NCTE).

Oliver, M. (2013). *The Social Model of Disability: Thirty Years on*. *Disability and Society*, *28*: 1024-1026.

Perner, D. and Porter, G. (2008). *'Creating Inclusive Schools: Changing roles and strategies'*. Research based Practices in Development Disabilities. *http://www.inclusion - Europe*

Rieser, R. (2013). *Teacher Education for Children with Disabilities*. Australia: UNICEF's REAP PROJ

Rouse, M. (2012). "Foreword", In: C. Forlin (Ed.) *Future Directions for Inclusive Teacher Education*. New York: Routledge.

Stubbs, S. (2011). 'An Overview of International Practice in Teacher Education for Inclusion'. UNICEF: A background paper.

UNESCO (2009). *Policy Guidelines on Inclusion in Education*. Paris: UNESCO.

UNICEF (2013). *The State of the World's Children 2013: Children with Disabilities*. UNICEF Publication.

WHO (2011). *World Report on Disability UK*: World Health Organisation.

Contributors

Dr. Sailaja Chennat is Associate Professor and senior Faculty in the Department of Education, University of Delhi, teaching at B.Ed., M.Ed., M.Phil. and Ph.D. levels. *Disability Studies* and *Inclusive Education* have been her primary areas of interest in teaching and research apart from *Research Methods* and *Teacher Education*. An edited volume on *E-Learning in Teacher Education: Experiences and Emerging Issues* (2014) and recent publication titled *Redefining Disability through Art* (August 2018) are part of her academic contributions. She has authored units of 'The Inclusive School' of B.Ed. curriculum of IGNOU and has been a core member and content editor of the RMSA module on Inclusive Education developed by NCERT.

Dr. Alka Behari is Senior Associate Professor at the Department of Education, the Central Institute of Education (CIE), University of Delhi, teaching at the B.Ed., M.Ed., M.Phil. and Ph.D. levels, for nearly thirty years. Her main areas of research interest are Teacher Education and Pedagogy, apart from Environment Studies and Inclusive Education. Along with Teaching, Dr. Behari has organised several Seminars and Workshops, and published in reputed journals and books. Her academic contributions, in the year 2018 include a Monograph titled, *Striving for excellence in Higher Education: Unfolding the Pedagogic Dimensions*, published by the Internal Quality Assurance Cell (IQAC), and training of about a thousand Undergraduate Teachers of the Non Collegiate Women's Education Board (NCWEB) of Delhi University in the area of Pedagogy.

Dr. Supriya Singh is working as Education consultant in an NGO Manzhi. She has been involved with research and teaching in the area of autism and has a doctoral degree from the University of Delhi, Department of Education. Her areas of interest are disabilities studies, inclusive practices and Education of children with autism.

Ms. Sangeeta Singh is currently working as an Assistant Professor in Lady Irwin College. University of Delhi. She holds a 'Diploma in Sign Language Interpreter Course' from Ali Yavar Jung National Institute of Speech and Hearing Disabilities (AYJNISHD), National Regional Centre. Her areas of interests are Science Education, Disability Studies and Inclusive Education.

Ms. Kavita Ghosh has a rich experience of working in schools at different grade levels and has also worked as a teacher-educator at the Department of Education. University of Delhi from where she is currently pursuing Ph.D., in education. Her interest areas include teacher education and reflective and inclusionary practices at both school and higher education levels.

Ms. Sumita Bhangu is a research scholar from Jamia Millia Islamia University. She has done B.Ed. and M.Ed. in Special Education (Learning Disabilities). She has worked with children with special needs in different schools of Delhi and NCR for six years.

Index